ARCTIC LANDS

ARCTIC LANDS

Baltic
Sea

Europe

OME

Black
Sea

ANCIENT
GREECE

Caspian
Sea

Mediterranean Sea

Asia

CHINA

Sea of Japan

JAPAN

NCIENT EGYPT

MESOPOTAMIA

Persian
Gulf

ANCIENT
INDIA

Red Sea

Arabian
Sea

Bay of
Bengal

South
China
Sea

Africa

Indian Ocean

Australia

Cape of Good Hope

POLITICS, SOCIETY & LEADERSHIP
through the ages

Series Editor Dr. John Haywood

LORENZ BOOKS

First published by Lorenz Books in 2001

© Anness Publishing Limited 2001

Published in the USA by Lorenz Books
Anness Publishing Inc.
27 West 20th Street
New York
NY 10011

Lorenz Books is an imprint of Anness Publishing Inc.

www.lorenzbooks.com

Publisher Joanna Lorenz
Manager, Children's Books, and Contributing Editor Gilly Cameron Cooper
Project Editor Rasha Elsaeed
Assistant Editor Sarah Uttridge
Editorial Reader Joy Wotton
Authors Daud Ali, Jen Green, Charlotte Hurdman, Fiona Macdonald, Lorna Oakes, Philip Steele, Michael Stotter, Richard Tames
Consultants Nick Allen, Cherry Alexander, Clara Bezanilla, Felicity Cobbing, Penny Dransart, Jenny Hall, Dr John Haywood, Dr Robin Holgate, Michael Johnson, Lloyd Laing, Jessie Lim, Heidi Potter, Louise Schofield, Leslie Webster, Designers Simon Borrough, Matthew Cook, John Jamieson, Joyce Mason, Caroline Reeves, Margaret Sadler, Alison Walker, Stuart Watkinson at Ideas Into Print, Sarah Williams
Special Photography John Freeman
Stylists Konika Shakar, Thomasina Smith, Melanie Williams
Production Controller: Claire Rae

Previously published as part of the *Step Into* series in 13 separate volumes:
Ancient Egypt, Ancient Greece, Ancient India, Ancient Japan, Aztec & Maya Worlds, Celtic World, Chinese Empire, Inca World, Mesopotamia, North American Indians, Roman Empire, Stone Age, Viking World.

PICTURE CREDITS
b=bottom, t=top, c=centre, l=left, r=right
AKG: 10tl, 14tr, 13tr, 15c, 30tl, 59br, 53tl, 54tl; Lesley and Roy Adkins: 41t; The Ancient Art and Architecture Collection Ltd:16r, 16-17, 18br, 35tl, 39tl, 44t, 52cl, 53cl, 57tr; Japan Archive: 27tr and cr, 29tr, 30br, 31tl, 31tr, 32bl, 33tr; The Bodleian Library: 51cl; The Bridgeman Art Library : 8bl, 9tr, 9br, 20cl, 21tr, 23c, 29tl, 36bl, 41b; The British Museum: 17t, 47b; Bildarchiv Preussischer Kulturbesitz: 11bl, 12tl, 15tl; Bulloz: 11br; C.M Dixon:8tl, 18t, 26tl, 36tr, 36br, 37tr , 37cl, 37br, 38l, 40bl, 42tl, 47t, 47cl, 48tl, 49bl, 49tr, 59bl; Musee Calvet, Avignon: 42br; Christies: 29bl; Peter Clayton: 19t, 19b, 35bl; Corbis-Bettman: 58tr; Corbis: 20tl, 23tl, 27tl, 60tl, 60bl, 60br, 61tr, 61cl, 61cr, 61b; Sylvia Corday: 9tl; E.T Archive (Art Archive): 21tl, 22tl, 25t, 25bl, 27br, 28bl, 48br, 51tl; Mary Evans Picture Library : 22c, 25br, 34tr, 38r; Werner Forman Archive: 24bl, 26bl, 29cr, 15bl, 43bl, 52tr, 55br, 56cl, 56tr; Robert Harding: 9bl, 12cr, 13cl; David Hawkins: 11t; Michael Holford: 18bl, 27br, 40tr, 40br, 44cl, 49br, 50br; The Hutchison Library: 28bl, 33bl, 33br; Michael Nicholson: 34tl, 35tr; National Museum of Wales: 43br; Peter Newark's Pictures: 58l, 59tl, 59tr; Andes Press Agency: 57tl; Mick Sharp: 44b, 45t, 47cr; South American Photo Library: 50tl, 51tr, 53tr, 55tl, 55tr, 57cl; Still Pictures: 54b; Tony Stone: 23tr; TRIP: 24br; University of Oslo: 46t; Visual Arts Library: 48br; Victoria and Albert Museum: 21c; York University Trust: 45l; Zefa: 16l, 17b, 24tr, 46b

10 9 8 7 6 5 4 3 2 1

CONTENTS

KEY
Look out for the border patterns used throughout this book. They will help you identify each culture.

The Stone Age   Japan   Aztec & Maya

Mesopotamia   Ancient Greece   Inca Empire

Ancient Egypt   Roman Empire   North American

India   The Celts   Indians

China   The Vikings

Keeping Control

Imagine what it would be like if there were no rules at school, or no one had ever told you how to behave or what to do! When human beings live or work together, they work out basic rules about how to behave. This saves arguing all the time, and makes sure that jobs for the good of everyone, such as cleaning, get done. Often, we can work out for ourselves how to be sociable – to behave with other people. But rules may also be made by leaders and teachers. Throughout history, there have been leaders who used their experience and wisdom to guide, teach and organize – or govern – others in the best possible way. There have also been many cruel and greedy tyrants whose interest lay in increasing their own power and wealth rather than the good of the people.

People live or work together at all sorts of different levels – from little groups such as your family or your class at school to the school itself and the community in which it lies. At each new level, there are additional sets of rules, and more leaders –

The first humans lived very simply, in small family groups. There were no chiefs or rulers. The leaders were the strongest and fittest. Each group was only concerned with survival.

The warrior kings of Mycenae in ancient Greece ruled from 1500BC. They lived in palaces enclosed by massive walls, called citadels. Administrators and the rest of the population lived outside the walls.

TIMELINE 8000BC–40BC

8000BC The farming way of life begins in the Middle East. People begin to settle down and live in villages. Differences in wealth and status emerge.

Cuneiform writing from Mesopotamia

3500BC The first cities develop in Mesopotamia. Each is an independent state with its own ruler.

3000BC The kingdom of Egypt is founded. Its rulers, or pharaohs, are believed to be living gods.

2600BC City-states develop in northern India.

One of over 750 hieroglyphic symbols in the Egyptian writing system

2350BC King Urukagina of Lagash in Mesopotamia issues the oldest known law code.

Chinese soldier of the Chou Dynasty

2000BC Ancesters of the modern Inuit arrive in Alaska from Siberia.

c.1792–1750BC Hammurabi of Babylon issues a law code about property and marriage.

1112BC Beginning of Chou Dynasty in China, during which emperors become known as 'Sons of Heaven'.

The Greek philosopher, Socrates

8000BC   3000BC   2000BC   750BC

from the grown-ups in a family and the teachers and principal in a school, to the president or prime minister of a country. A number of people organized in this way is called society. Through history, society has become more and more complex as populations have grown. In this book you will be able to see how society evolved in different ways around the world, and how the leaders in various cultures and civilizations, controlled or governed their peoples.

In the beginning, it was all very simple. In prehistoric times, people hunted animals and picked plants for food. There was rarely any food to spare. A few related families lived together in small bands called clans.

Viking communities were at first small and tribal, hemmed in by high mountains. Land for big settlements to develop was limited. Some Viking chieftains conquered other tribes and built up kingdoms.

Everyone knew one another, and looked to the oldest and most experienced people in the clan for advice and decisions. Where there was water and fertile land, though, people learned how to farm and began to settle in permanent homes. Some farmers were more successful than others. They could use their wealth to control or persuade others. In this way, differences of status or rank developed. The Celts, for example, were made up of many tribes, each of which

Among tribal peoples, such as the Celts and Vikings, fighting for new land was a way of life and survival. Their warriors were important and respected members of tribal society. Those who were good at leading people often became chieftans.

750BC Celtic chiefdoms develop in central Europe.

680–627BC The Assyrian Empire is at its greatest extent.

594BC Athenian statesman Solon reforms the laws of Athens.

509–507BC Democratic government is introduced in Athens.

509BC The Romans overthrow their king and create a republic.

A triumphal arch, built to celebrate a Roman victory

c.300BC Maya city-states develop in Mesoamerica.

221BC Qin Shi Huangdi becomes the first emperor of China.

58–52BC The Roman commander Julius Caesar conquers the Celts of Gaul (modern France).

44BC Julius Caesar destroys the Roman republic when he appoints himself dictator for life. He is murdered soon afterward.

500BC   **300BC**   **40BC**

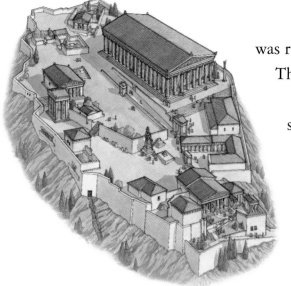

was ruled by a chief. Below the chief came warriors and then priests. Then came the farmers and last of all, the unpaid slave labor.

Although they were powerful, chiefs and kings in these simple societies had to listen to their followers or they lost their support. Like many other rulers throughout history, Celtic leaders rewarded their warriors with gifts to keep them loyal.

The Celtic tribes were scattered, and remained small and clan-based. In the fertile valleys of big rivers in the Middle East, China, India and Egypt, though, there were the resources, the climate and the space for settlements to expand.

Encouraging belief in powerful gods was one way of keeping citizens in order. In Athens, temples to the guardian god Athena dominated the city from the rocky Acropolis. Many public festivals were held there.

Great cities, with populations of tens of thousands, and a huge range of peoples and skills, grew up. Organizing such large communities was far too much for the ruler alone. Administrators, clerks and specialist advisers were needed to help decide how their cities and lands should be run. These groups of rulers and advisers were the first governments.

Rulers of early civilizations and cultures had to work hard at holding on to their power. The kings of city-states in Mesopotamia, the pharaohs of ancient Egypt and the Incas of South America promoted the idea that they were appointed by the gods, or even took on godly status themselves. Many leaders

In the Islamic world, it was not only scholars like these who had to study. Every Muslim had to learn the Arabic language so that they could read the laws laid down in the Koran.

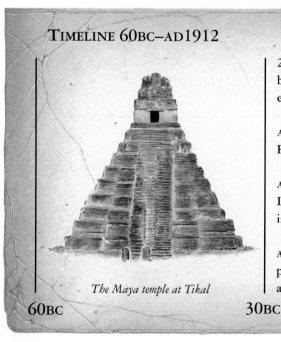

TIMELINE 60BC–AD1912

The Maya temple at Tikal

27BC Augustus becomes the first emperor of Rome.

AD476 Fall of the Roman Empire.

AD593–622 Imperial government is introduced in Japan.

AD793 Viking pirates attack Britain and Ireland.

A Japanese samurai warrior

AD800–900 Maya city-states collapse after an environmental disaster.

AD930 Viking settlers found the Icelandic Althing (national assembly).

1185 The Japanese emperor falls under the domination of the shoguns (military commanders).

Spanish doubloons, made from the gold they found in the Americas

60BC   30BC   AD800   1200

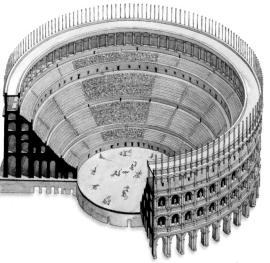

Roman emperors staged increasingly bloodthirsty gladiatorial games in the Colosseum in Rome. The events showed off the emperor's power and impressed the people. The stadium held up to 50,000 spectators.

ruled by fear, threatening dreadful punishments if they were disobeyed. Others won over those who might be useful by handing out riches, land or status.

Mesopotamian rulers were among the first to issue a formal set of rules, or laws, which the inhabitants of their city-states had to follow. The laws were inscribed on stone pillars – together with the punishments for breaking them – and erected in public places so that everyone could see them.

Those who made the rules were the few – the rich, the powerful or those who had inherited leadership from their fathers before them. The ordinary citizen did not have a say in how society was run. Then the Athenian Greeks introduced the idea of democracy, a system of government that allowed members of the community to vote. Most governments in the Western world today are democratically elected (chosen). The Romans developed a type of government called a republic. The United States and France are two countries that are run as republics today with democratically elected representatives. You can look at the different forms of government around the world today, and then see how they began and developed through history.

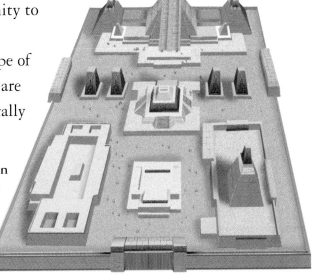

Maya rulers were buried in temple complexes. Each ruler aimed to build a fine temple as a memorial to his reign. The complex included areas for playing ball games.

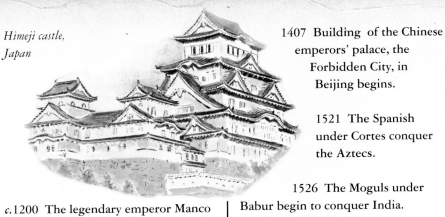

Himeji castle, Japan

c.1200 The legendary emperor Manco Capac founds the Inca Empire.

1325 Foundation of the Aztec Empire.

1407 Building of the Chinese emperors' palace, the Forbidden City, in Beijing begins.

1521 The Spanish under Cortes conquer the Aztecs.

1526 The Moguls under Babur begin to conquer India.

1532 The Spanish under Pizarro conquer the Incas.

1687 Mogul empire reachest its peak under Aurangzeb.

1868 In Japan the shogunate falls and the emperors are returned to power.

1912 China becomes a republic after the last emperor is deposed.

Body of aChinese princess in a jade suit

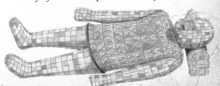

1400   1600   1912

Beginnings of Social Structure

Iɴ Sᴛᴏɴᴇ Aɢᴇ ᴛɪᴍᴇs, there were very few people in the world. Experts estimate that the world's population in 13,000ʙᴄ was about eight million. Today it is nearly six billion – 750 *thousand* times as many. We can guess how Stone Age people lived together by looking at hunter-gatherer societies that still exist today in South America and the Pacific.

Groups of families lived together in clans. All the members of each clan were related to each other, usually through their mother's family or by marriage. Clans were large enough to protect and feed everyone, but not so large that they were unmanageable. All the members of a clan, including children, were involved in finding and gathering food for everyone. Clans were probably also part of larger tribes, which may have met up at certain times of year, such as for a summer hunt. The members of a tribe shared a language and a way of life. When people learned how to farm, populations increased and societies began to be organized in more complicated ways.

Mᴏᴛʜᴇʀ Gᴏᴅᴅᴇssᴇs
Eight thousand years ago, this clay sculpture from Turkey may have been worshipped as a goddess of motherhood. Families were often traced through the female line because mothers give birth, so everyone knew who the babies belonged to. The fathers were not always known.

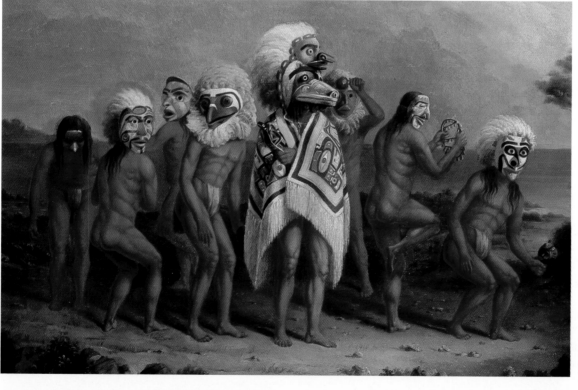

Sʜᴀᴍᴀɴ Lᴇᴀᴅᴇʀs
This painting from the 1800s shows Native American shamans performing a ritual dance. Shamans were the spiritual leaders of their tribes. They knew the dances, chants, prayers and ceremonies that would bring good luck and please the spirits. Shamanism is found in hunter-gatherer societies around the world today and was practiced in prehistoric times.

TRIBAL CHIEF

This man is a Zulu chief from South Africa. His higher rank is shown by what he wears. In prehistoric times, tribes might have been ruled by chiefs or councils of elders. An old man buried at Sungir in Russia around 23,000BC was probably a chief. His body was found richly decorated with fox teeth and beads made of mammoth ivory.

SCENES FROM LONG AGO

Paintings on cliff walls in the Sahara Desert in Africa show hippopotamuses being hunted and herders tending cattle. Other images show a woman pounding flour, ceremonies and a family with a dog. They show that, in 6000BC, it was a fertile area with organized communities.

FINE FIGURE

Between 3000 and 2000BC, some of the finest prehistoric sculpture was made on the Cycladic Islands of Greece. This figurine is made of ground marble and shows a slender woman with her arms folded above her waist. Finely worked sculpture was a sign that a society had become more complex than a simple clan. There were more people with more specialized jobs, and more free time.

A TRADITIONAL WAY OF LIFE

The man on the right is helping a boy prepare for his coming-of-age ceremony in Papua New Guinea. Traditional ways of life are still strong in that country, where there are many remote tribes. In some villages, all the men live together, rather than with their wives and children. This allows them to organize their work, such as hunting, more easily.

Legendary Kings of Mesopotamia

FROM AROUND 3000BC, the people of Mesopotamia lived in walled cities. Each city had its own ruler and guardian god. The rulers wanted to be remembered forever, by the wonderful temples and palaces they had built, or by having their deeds and battle victories carved into stone pillars called stelae.

Some of the world's oldest stories are about Gilgamesh, king of one of Sumer's most important cities in around 2700BC. Stories and poems about him passed from the Sumerian people to those who lived in the Babylonian and Assyrian empires. Finally, in the 7th century BC, the Assyrians wrote down all these exciting stories onto clay tablets. The *Epic of Gilgamesh* was stored in the great libraries of King Ashurbanipal of Assyria, where it was discovered by archaeologists over 100 years ago. Gilgamesh was not a good king at first, so the gods created Enkidu, a wild, hairy man, to fight him. The king realized he had met his match, and the two then became good friends and went everywhere together.

GIANT ATTACK
The giant Humbaba guarded the Cedar Forest, far away, in Lebanon. His voice was like thunder, his breath was fire, and he could hear the faintest noise from the ends of the earth. To test their courage, Gilgamesh and Enkidu decided to kill this monster. They were terrified by the giant's dreadful face and taunting words, but finally cut off his head with one stroke.

THE BULL OF HEAVEN
Ishtar, the goddess of love and war (on the left), tries to stop Enkidu and Gilgamesh from killing the Bull of Heaven. Ishtar had fallen in love with the hero-king, and she wanted to marry him. Gilgamesh knew that the goddess was fickle, and turned her down. Ishtar was furious and asked her father, Anu the sky god, to give her the Bull of Heaven so she could take revenge on Gilgamesh. The Bull was a deadly beast who had the power to bring death and long-term misery to the city of Uruk. The two friends fought and killed the bull. Enkidu (on the right) hung on to its tail, as Gilgamesh delivered the death blow with his sword.

THE CITY OF URUK

There is very little of Uruk left today, but it was a very important city when Gilgamesh was king. The city had splendid temples dedicated to Anu, the sky god, and his daughter Ishtar who fell in love with Gilgamesh. The king also built a great wall around the city. When his friend Enkidu died, Gilgamesh was heartbroken, and also frightened because he realized he would die one day, too. He wanted to live forever. In the end, he decided that creating a beautiful city was his best chance of immortality. He would be remembered forever for creating the fine temples and massive walls of Uruk.

THE PLANT OF ETERNAL LIFE

This massive stone carving of a heroic figure found in the palace of King Sargon II may be of Gilgamesh. Sargon II created the world's first empire by conquering all the cities of Sumer, Mari and Ebla. Gilgamesh set out to find Utnapishtim, the ruler of another Sumerian city who was said to have found the secret of eternal life. The way was long and dangerous, and led into the mountains where lions prowled. After a terrifying walk in total darkness, Gilgamesh emerged on the other side of the mountain into the garden of the gods. Beyond the garden were the Waters of Death, but our hero found a ferryman to take him safely across. At last he met Utnapishtim, who told him he would never die if he found a plant that grew on the sea bed. Gilgamesh tied stones on his feet, dived into the sea and picked the plant. However, on the way home, he stooped down to drink at a pool. A water snake appeared and snatched the plant. With it went Gilgamesh's hope of immortality.

LASTING FAME

The figures on this stone vase from Uruk probably show Gilgamesh. The king found the lasting fame he wanted because his name lived on in stories and legends, and in statues and carvings such as this.

Kingly Duties in Mesopotamia

THE KINGS OF MESOPOTAMIA considered themselves to have been chosen by the gods. For example, Ur-Nanshe of Lagash (2480BC) said that he was granted kingship by Enlil, chief of the gods, and Ashurbanipal (669BC) claimed he was the son of the Assyrian god, Ashur, and his wife, Belit. The Mesopotamian kings ran the state on the god's behalf. Even in the Assyrian Empire, when the kings had grand titles such as "King of the Universe," they still felt they were responsible to the gods for the well-being of their people. Another of their titles was "Shepherd." This meant they had to look after their people, just as a shepherd tends his flock.

AUTHORITY
An onyx mace was carried by the Babylonian kings of Mesopotamia as a symbol of authority. At New Year, the king laid the mace before the statue of the chief god, Marduk. When he picked it up again, it meant he would reign for another year.

SUN GOD TABLET FROM SIPPAR
Kings had to see that temples and statues of the gods were kept in good repair. This tablet shows King Nabu-apla-iddina of Babylon being led into the presence of the god Shamash. The story on the tablet tells us that the king wanted to make a new statue of the god. He was meant to repair the old one but it had been stolen by enemies. Fortunately a priest found a model of the statue that could be copied.

MAKE A FLY WHISK
You will need: calico fabric, pencil, ruler, Elmer's glue and brush, scissors, thick card, paints and paintbrushes, newspaper.

1 Draw long leaf shapes about 1½ ft long on to the calico fabric with the pencil. Paint the shapes with watered down Elmer's glue. Leave to dry.

2 Cut out the leaf shapes. Make a card spine for the center of each leaf as shown, thicker at the bottom than at the top, and glue them on.

3 Paint the leaves in gold, yellow and red paints on both sides. Add fine detail by cutting carefully into the edge of each leaf using the scissors.

FIGHTING FOR THE GODS

Kings believed that they were commanded by the gods to conquer other cities and states in their name. In this relief, King Sennacherib is sitting on his throne receiving the booty and prisoners taken after the city of Lachish had fallen. The king devoted a whole room in his palace at Nineveh to the story of this siege. He also made war on Babylon and completely devastated the city. In 612BC the Babylonians had their revenge. They destroyed the city of Nineveh and hacked out Sennacherib's face on this sculpture.

EXPLORATION AND DISCOVERY

Another mark of good kingship was the expansion of knowledge. King Shalmaneser III sent an expedition to find the source of the River Tigris (pictured here). His men set up a stela (a carved monument) to record the discovery and made offerings to the gods to celebrate. Many Mesopotamian kings were learned men. They collected clay tablets to make great libraries or built up collections of exotic plants and animals.

Fly whisks made of long thin leaves or feathery reeds kept the flies away from the king. They could also be used as a fan to keep him cool.

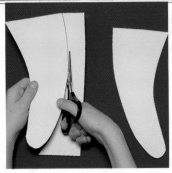

4 Draw two identical handle shapes on to the stiff card. They should be about 8½ in long and 4 in wide at the top. Cut out the shapes with the scissors.

5 Tear up newspaper strips and dip into glue. Wrap the strips around the edges of the two handles to fasten them together. Leave the top of the handle unglued.

6 Decorate the handle with gold paint. Leave to dry. Paint decorative details on to the gold with black paint using a fine paintbrush.

7 Glue the bottoms of the leaves and push them into the top of the handle, between the two pieces of cardboard. Spread the leaves well apart.

Running the Assyrian Empire

FROM THE BEGINNING of the 800s BC, the country of Assyria in the north of Mesopotamia began to grow into a vast empire. The land was divided into provinces that were named after the main city, such as Nineveh, Samaria or Damascus. Every city had a governor who made sure that taxes were collected, called up soldiers in times of war, and supplied workers when a new palace or temple was to be built. The governor made sure that merchants could travel safely, and he was also responsible for law and order. If the king and his army passed through the province, the governor supplied them with food and drink. A vast system of roads connected the king's palace with governors' residences and the important cities of the Empire.

ENFORCED REMOVAL
Conquered people were banished from their homelands, and forced to go and live in Assyria. These people were from Lachish, near Jerusalem, and were moved to the Assyrian city of Nineveh. The men were used as forced labor in the limestone quarries.

THE KING'S MEN
An Assyrian king was constantly surrounded by bodyguards, astrologers and other members of the court. There were also visitors such as provincial governors who helped the king run the Empire. The King's servants included scribes to write down orders, messengers to deliver them and an attendant to hold a parasol. In this picture King Ashurnasirpal is celebrating a successful bull hunt with priests and musicians.

MAKE A PARASOL
You will need: pencil, colored card 2 ft x 2 ft, scissors, masking tape, paints in bright colors and paintbrushes, white card, string or twine, glue, dowel.

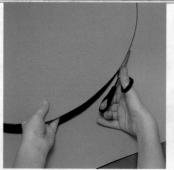

1 Draw a circle on the colored card measuring roughly 2 ft across. Cut out the circle with the scissors keeping the edge as neat as possible.

2 Cut a slit from the edge of the circle to the center. Pull one edge of the slit over the other to make a conical shape. Secure with masking tape.

3 Paint your parasol with red paint. Leave to dry. Then paint stripes in lots of different shades of orange and red from the top to the bottom.

TOWARD A NEW LIFE

Defeated people camp out en route to a new life in Assyria. The Assyrian Empire grew so big, that it could take months to travel back from a newly won territory. Conquered people were usually kept together in families and given homes in the countryside. Often they were set to work to cultivate more land.

KEEPING ACCOUNTS

Assyrian scribes at the governor's palace at Til Barsip on the River Euphrates make a note of taxes demanded by the king. Taxes were exacted not only from the local Assyrian people, but also from the conquered territories. They could be paid in produce, such as grain, horses or cattle, and wine.

Kings were accompanied by an attendant carrying a sunshade, which was probably made of fine woolen material and decorated with tassels.

USEFUL TRIBUTE

Conquered people had to give tributes such as horses to the Assyrian king, as well as food for the animals. The horses swelled the chariot and cavalry units in the Assyrian army. The best-bred and strongest horses came from the foothills of the Zagros Mountains to the east of Assyria.

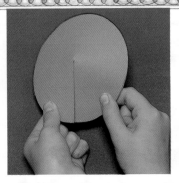

4 Cut 20 oval shapes about 2 in by 1½ in from the white card. Cover with a base colour of gold. Leave to dry, then paint with bright designs.

5 Use the scissors to make holes around the edge of the parasol and in the ovals. Attach the ovals to the parasol with twine, knotting it as shown.

6 Cut a small circle out of colored card measuring 4 in across. Make a slit to the center, and pull one edge over the other as before. Paint the small cone gold.

7 Glue it to the top of the parasol. Paint the handle with gold paint and allow to dry. Attach it to the inside of the parasol using plenty of masking tape.

The Pharaohs of Egypt

THE CROOK AND FLAIL
These emblems of the god Osiris became badges of royal authority. The crook stood for kingship and the flail for the fertility of the land.

flail

crook

THE WORD PHARAOH comes from the Egyptian *per-aa*, which meant "great house" or "palace." It later came to mean the man who lived in the palace, the ruler. Pictures and statues show pharaohs with special badges of royalty, such as crowns, headcloths, false beards, scepters and a crook and flail held in each hand. The pharaoh was the most important person in Egypt. He was the link between the people and their gods, and therefore had to be protected and cared for. The pharaoh's life was busy. He was high priest, chief law-maker, commander of the army and in charge of the country's wealth. He had to be a clever politician, too. The ancient Egyptians believed that on his death, the pharaoh became a god. Pharaohs were usually men, but women sometimes ruled Egypt as Queen Hatshepsut did, when her husband Thutmose II died and his son was still a child. A pharaoh could take several wives. Within royal families, it was common for fathers to marry daughters and for brothers to marry sisters. Sometimes pharaohs married foreign princesses in order to make an alliance with another country.

MOTHER GODDESS OF THE PHARAOHS
Hathor was worshipped as the mother goddess of each pharaoh. Here she is shown welcoming the pharaoh Horemheb to the afterlife. Horemheb was a nobleman who became a brilliant military commander. He was made pharaoh in 1323BC.

MAKE A CROWN

You will need: 2 sheets of A1 card (red and white), pencil, ruler, scissors, masking tape, cardboard roll, bandage, pva glue and brush, acrylic paint (white, gold), brush, beads, skewer, water pot and brush.

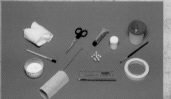

White crown of Upper Egypt

6¼ in

40cm

3 in

21 in

8 in

Snake

6 in

22 in

Red crown of Lower Egypt

Mark out these patterns on to your card. Cut around them with scissors.

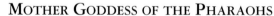

1 Bend the shape made from the white card into a cylinder, as shown. Use lengths of masking tape to join the two edges together firmly.

RAMSES MEETS THE GODS

This painting shows the dead pharaoh Ramses I meeting the gods Horus (left) and Anubis (right). Pharaohs had to pass safely through the afterlife. If they did not, the link between the gods and the world would be broken forever.

THE QUEEN'S TEMPLE

This great temple (*below*) was built in honor of Queen Hatshepsut. It lies at the foot of towering cliffs at Deir el-Bahri, on the west bank of the Nile near the Valley of the Kings. The queen had the temple built as a place for her body to be prepared for burial. Pyramids, tombs and temples were important symbols of power in Egypt. By building this temple, Hatshepsut wanted people to remember her as a pharaoh in her own right.

HATSHEPSUT

A female pharaoh was so unusual that pictures of Queen Hatshepsut show her with all the badges of a male king, including a false beard! Here she wears the pharaoh's crown. The cobra on the front of the crown is the badge of Lower Egypt.

The double crown worn by the pharaohs was called the pschent. *It symbolized the unification of the two kingdoms. The white section at the top (hedjet) stood for Upper Egypt, and the red section at the bottom (deshret) for Lower Egypt.*

2 Tape a cardboard roll into the hole at the top. Plug its end with a ball of bandage. Tape the bandage in position and glue down the edges.

3 Wrap the white section with lengths of bandage. Paint over these with an equal mixture of white paint and glue. Leave the crown in a warm place to dry.

4 Now take the shape made from the red card. Wrap it tightly around the white section, as shown, joining the edges with masking tape.

5 Now paint the snake gold, sticking on beads as eyes. When dry, score lines across its body. Bend the snake's body and glue it to the crown, as shown.

THE PHARAOHS OF EGYPT   17

High Society in Egypt

EGYPTIAN PALACES were vast complexes. They included splendid public buildings where the pharaoh met foreign rulers and carried out important ceremonies. Members of the royal family lived in luxury in beautiful townhouses with painted walls and tiled floors near the palace.

The governors of Egypt's regions also lived like princes, and pharaohs had to be careful that they did not become too rich and powerful. The royal court included large numbers of officials and royal advisors. There were lawyers, architects, tax officials, priests and army officers. The most important court official of all was the vizier, who carried out many of the pharaoh's duties for him.

The officials and nobles were at the top of Egyptian society. But most of the hard work that kept the country running smoothly was carried out by merchants and craft workers, by farmers, laborers and slaves.

GREAT LADIES
Ahmose-Nefertari was the wife of Ahmose I. She carries a lotus flower and a flail. Kings could take many wives. It was common for them to have a harem of beautiful women.

A NOBLEMAN AND HIS WIFE
This limestone statue shows an unknown couple from Thebes. The man may have worked in a well-respected profession, as a doctor, government official or engineer. Noblewomen did not work but were quite independent. Any property that a wife brought into her marriage remained hers.

THE SPLENDORS OF THE COURT
This is the throne room of Ramses III's palace at Medinet Habu, on the west bank of the Nile near Thebes. Pharaohs often had many palaces, and Medinet Habu was one of Ramses III's lesser ones. Surviving fragments of tiles and furniture give us an idea of just how splendid the royal court must have been. A chamber to one side of the throne room is even believed to be an early version of a shower cubicle!

RELAXATION

Ankherhau (*above*), a wealthy overseer of workmen, relaxes at home with his wife. They are listening to a harpist. Life was pleasant for those who could afford it. Kings and nobles had dancers, musicians and acrobats to entertain them. Cooks worked in their kitchens preparing sumptuous meals. By comparison, ordinary people ate simple food, rarely eating meat except for the small animals they caught themselves.

HAIR CARE

The royal family was waited on by domestic servants who attended to their every need. Here (*left*), the young Queen Kawit, wife of the pharaoh Mentuhotep II, has her hair dressed by her personal maid. Although many of the female servants employed in wealthy households were slaves, a large number of servants were free. This meant that they had the right to leave their employer at any time.

Rulers of India

DISPLAY OF POWER
A Mogul emperor rides through the city on top of an elephant, a symbol of royalty. Kings often processed through their cities to display their power and majesty. They were always followed by attendants and courtiers.

Oᴠᴇʀ ᴛʜᴇ ᴄᴇɴᴛᴜʀɪᴇs, India has been ruled by leaders from many different lands, cultures and religions. Their titles and the symbolic objects that surrounded them are often a clue to their roles and beliefs. From the time of the emperor Ashoka, around 250ʙᴄ, the ruler became known as *cakravartin* (wheel-turner). The wheel was a Buddhist symbol for the world, so this suggested that the king made the world go around. Objects that were symbols of royalty included scepters, crowns and yak-tail fans. The most important object was the *chatra* (umbrella), which signified the king's protection of his realm. Hindu *maharajadhirajas* (kings) developed the idea that the god Vishnu lived within them. When Islam arrived in the 1300s, the sultans showed their obedience to the caliph (the head of Islam in Baghdad) by taking titles such as *nasir* (helper). Rulers in the Mogul Empire (1526–1857), took Persian titles such as *padshah* (emperor).

THE MARKS OF A KING
A picture of the foot of Hindu ruler Rama bears images of a lotus, conch shell, umbrella, fly whisk and other royal symbols. People believed that a world-ruling king was born with features such as these on their soles and palms. Rama was said to be a wise and good ruler. He was later deified (made into a god).

MAKE A CHAURI

You will need: strip of corrugated cardboard measuring 1 in x 10 in, raffia, scissors, Scotch tape, Elmer's glue, 8 in length of dowel, modeling clay, paint in gold and a contrasting color, paintbrushes, foil candy wrappers.

1 Put the strip of card on a covered, flat surface. Cut strips of raffia. Carefully tape the strands of raffia to the card. Leave your chauri to dry.

2 Wrap the card and raffia around the dowel, and glue it in place. Keep the card ¾ in from the top, so that the dowel supports the raffia.

3 Tape the card and raffia band firmly in place to make sure that it will not come undone when you use your whisk. Leave the whisk to dry.

A KING'S HALO

The king in this procession has a halo surrounding his head. From Mogul times, rulers were thought to be blessed with the divine light of wisdom. This was represented in pictures by a halo.

ROYAL CUSHION

Raja Ram Singh of Jodhpur sits with his nobles. Only the king was allowed to sit on a cushion. The Rajputs were kings of northern India who fought against Muslim invaders in the first millennium AD. In the Mogul Empire, they were important military allies of the Muslims.

ROYAL RAMA

Rama was a Hindu king, believed to be the earthly representative of the god Vishnu. He is with his wife Sita and his brothers. He holds a bow, a symbol of courage. Attendants hold other symbols of royalty.

The fly whisk was a symbol of a Hindu king's power.

4 Make lots of small beads from modeling clay. Glue these on to the dowel in a circle, about 1 in below the strip of card. Leave to dry.

5 Paint the dowel and beads with two coats of gold paint. Leave it to dry. Then paint a pattern on the strip of card and the dowel, in different colors.

6 When the paint is dry, glue bits of colored foil paper to your chauri. The more decorations you add, the more it will look like a real chauri.

The Mogul Empire

ORDERLY COURTIERS
Mogul nobles had to take part in court rituals. They had to arrive punctually at court, and line up in rows. Dress and posture were very important. The cummerbund tied around the waist and the turban were signs of self-control. Courtiers guarded the palace strictly in turn.

THE FIRST MOGUL EMPEROR
Babur defeats Ibrahim Lodi, the last sultan of Delhi, at the Battle of Panipat in 1526. Babur invaded India because he was unable to recapture his own homeland in Samarkand.

IN 1526, A PRINCE called Babur invaded India from the north-west. He swept across the country with a powerful army and soon arrived in Delhi. The city was the heart of the Sultanate, the kingdom that Islamic invaders had founded 300 years before. Babur defeated the Sultanate and founded the Mogul Empire. It was the last important dynasty of India before the British arrived in the 1700s.

Babur's grandson, Akbar was a great Mogul leader from 1556 to 1605. Although a Muslim, he was tolerant of other religions and took Hindu princesses as his wives. Forty years later, the warlike Mogul ruler Aurangzeb returned to a stricter form of Islam and expanded the Empire. The Moguls were patrons of the arts, and built glorious palaces, gardens

and tombs. Many of India's most precious works of art date from this era. Persian was the language of their court, but they also spoke Urdu, a mixture of Persian, Arabic and Hindi.

MAKE A LACQUERED STORAGE BOX

You will need: pencil, ruler, sheets of card, scissors, Scotch tape, newspaper, wallpaper paste or flour and water, bowl, fine sandpaper, paint in white and bright colors, paintbrushes, non-toxic varnish.

1 Scale up the shape shown here to the size you want your box to be and copy the shape on to card. Cut out the shape and fix the edges with Scotch tape to form a box.

2 Draw 4 card triangles with sides the same length as the top of the box. Tape the triangles together to form a pyramid and cut off the top.

3 Add newspaper strips to the paste, or flour and water, to make papier-mâché. Cover the box and lid with three layers of papier-mâché. Dry between layers.

A POEM IN STONE

The Mogul emperor Shah Jahan commemorated his wife Mumtaz Mahal (who died in childbirth) by building this magnificent mausoleum. It was built between 1631 and 1648, and came to be known as the Taj Mahal. It is built of white marble from Rajasthan. The Taj Mahal is one of the most magnificent buildings in the world, and is the high point of Mogul art.

JADE HOOKAH

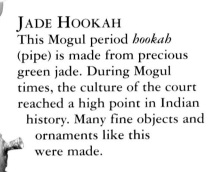

This Mogul period *hookah* (pipe) is made from precious green jade. During Mogul times, the culture of the court reached a high point in Indian history. Many fine objects and ornaments like this were made.

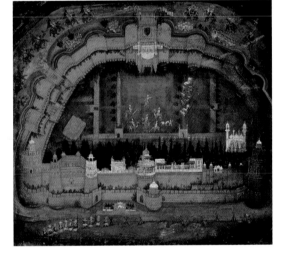

Lacquered boxes were popular with women of the royal court for storing jewelry.

RED PALACE

The Red Fort in Agra is one of the palaces built by Akbar. The Mogul emperors broke with the tradition of kings living in tents, and built sumptuous residences in their capital cities.

4 When the papier-mâché is dry, smooth any rough edges with sandpaper. Add squares of cardboard as feet. Paint the box and the lid white.

5 Allow the painted box and lid to dry. Draw a pattern on to the box and lid. You could copy the pattern shown here, or use your own design.

6 Paint the lid and the box, including the feet, with brightly colored paints. Use the pattern that you have drawn as a guide. Leave to dry.

7 To finish, paint the box and lid with a coat of non-toxic varnish. Leave to dry completely, then add a final coat of varnish. Your storage box is now finished.

Lives of the Chinese Rulers

THE FIRST CHINESE RULERS lived about 4,000 years ago. This early dynasty (period of rule) was known as the Xia. We know little about the Xia rulers, because Chinese history of this time is mixed up with ancient myths and legends. Excavations have told us more about the Shang Dynasty rulers about 1,000 years later. They were waited on by slaves and had fabulous treasures.

During the next period of rule, the Chou Dynasty, an idea grew up that Chinese rulers were Sons of Heaven, placed on the throne by the will of the gods. After China became a powerful, united empire in 221BC, this idea helped keep the emperors in power. Rule of the Empire was passed down from father to son. Anyone who seized the throne by force had to show that the overthrown ruler had offended the gods. Earthquakes and natural disasters were often taken as signs of the gods' displeasure.

Chinese emperors were among the world's most powerful rulers ever. Emperors of China's last dynasty, the Ching (1644–1912), lived in luxurious palaces that were cut off from the world. When they traveled through the streets, the common people had to stay indoors.

WHERE EMPERORS PRAYED
There are beautifully decorated pillars inside the Hall of Prayer for Good Harvests at Tiantan in Beijing. An emperor was a religious leader as well as a political ruler. Each New Year, the emperor arrived at the hall at the head of a great procession. The evening was spent praying to the gods for a plentiful harvest in the coming year.

TO THE HOLY MOUNTAIN
This stele (inscribed stone) is located on the summit of China's holiest mountain, Taishan, in Shandong province. To the ancient Chinese, Taishan was the home of the gods. For over 2,000 years the emperors climbed the carved steps to the temple to offer prayers.

IN THE FORBIDDEN CITY
The vast Imperial Palace in Beijing is best described as "a city within a city." It was built between 1407 and 1420 by hundreds of thousands of laborers under the command of Emperor Yongle. Behind its high, red walls and moats were 800 beautiful halls and temples, set among gardens, courtyards and bridges. No fewer than 24 emperors lived here in incredible luxury, set apart from their subjects. The Imperial Palace was also known as the Forbidden City. Ordinary Chinese people were not even allowed to approach its gates.

"WE POSSESS ALL THINGS"

This was the message sent from Emperor Qianlong to the British King George III in 1793. Here the emperor is being presented with a gift of fine horses from the Kyrgyz people of Central Asia. By the late 1800s, Chinese rule took in Mongolia, Tibet and Central Asia. All kinds of fabulous gifts were sent to the emperor from every corner of the Empire, as everyone wanted to win his favor.

RITUALS AND CEREMONIES

During the Ching Dynasty, an emperor's duties included many long ceremonies and official receptions. Here in Beijing's Forbidden City, a long carpet leads to the ruler's throne. Officials in silk robes line the steps and terraces, holding their banners and ceremonial umbrellas high. Courtiers kneel and bow before the emperor. Behavior at the royal court was set out in the greatest detail. Rules decreed which kind of clothes could be worn and in which colors.

CARRIED BY HAND

The first Chinese emperor, Qin Shi Huangdi, is carried to a monastery high in the mountains in the 200s BC. He rides in a litter (a type of chair) that is carried on his servants' shoulders. Emperors always traveled with a large following of guards and courtiers.

Japan's Emperors of the Sun

THE JAPANESE PEOPLE began to live in villages in about 300BC. Over the next 600 years, the richest and most powerful of these villages became the centers of small kingdoms, controlling the surrounding lands. By about AD300, a kingdom based on the Yamato Plain in south-central Japan became bigger and stronger than the rest. It was ruled by chiefs of an *uji* (clan) who claimed to be descended from the Sun goddess. The chiefs of the Sun-clan were not only army commanders. They were priests, governors, law-makers and controllers of their people's treasure and food supply as well. Over the years, their powers increased.

By around AD500, Sun-clan chiefs from Yamato ruled over most of Japan. They claimed power as emperors, and organized lesser chiefs to work for them, giving them noble titles as a reward. Each emperor chose his own successor from within the Sun-clan, and handed over the sacred symbols of imperial power – a jewel, a mirror and a sword. If a male successor to the throne was too young to rule, an empress might act for a time as regent.

Descendants of these early emperors still rule Japan today, although their role is purely ceremonial. In other periods of Japan's history, too, the emperors had very little power. Some did play an active part in politics, while others spent their time shut away from the outside world.

HANIWA FIGURE
From around AD300-550, clay *haniwa* figures were put around tombs. Statues of soldiers, servants and animals were placed in an emperor's tomb to look after him in his next life.

NARA
This shrine is in the ancient city of Nara. Originally called Heijokyo, Nara was founded by Empress Gemmei (ruled AD707–715) as a new capital for her court. The city was planned and built in Chinese style, with streets arranged in a grid pattern. The Imperial Palace was situated at the northern edge.

FANTASTIC STORIES

Prince Shotoku (AD574–622) was descended from the imperial family and from another powerful clan, the Soga. He never became emperor, but ruled as regent for 30 years on behalf of Empress Suiko. Many fantastic stories were told about him. One was that he was able to speak as soon as he was born. It was also said that he could see into the future. More accurate reports of Shotoku's achievements list his introduction of a new calendar, and his reform of government, based on Chinese ideas. He was also a supporter of the new Buddhist faith, introduced from China.

LARGEST WOODEN STRUCTURE

The Hall of the Great Buddha at Nara was founded on the orders of Emperor Shomu in AD745. The whole temple complex is said to be the largest wooden structure in the world. It houses a bronze statue of the Buddha, 52 ft tall and weighing 550 tons. It was also designed to display the emperor's wealth and power. There is a treasury close to the Hall of the Great Buddha, built in AD756. This housed the belongings of Emperor Shomu and his wife, Empress Komyo. The treasury still contains many rare and valuable items.

BURIAL MOUNDS

The Yamato emperors were buried in huge, mound-shaped tombs surrounded by lakes. The largest, built for Emperor Nintoku, is 525 yd long. From above, the tombs have a keyhole-shaped layout. Inside, they contain many buried treasures.

THE SUN GODDESS

The Sun goddess Amaterasu Omikami is shown emerging from the earth in this print. She was both honored and feared by Japanese farmers. One of the emperor's tasks was to act as a link between the goddess and his people, asking for her help on their behalf. The goddess's main shrine was at Ise, in central Japan. Some of its buildings were designed to look like grain stores – a reminder of the Sun's power to cause a good or a bad harvest.

Keeping Control in Japan

IN EARLY JAPAN, everyone, from the proudest chief to the poorest peasant, owed loyalty to the emperor. However, many nobles ignored the emperor's orders – especially when they were safely out of reach of his court. There were plots and secret schemes as rival nobles struggled to influence the emperor or even to seize power for themselves.

Successive emperors passed laws to try to keep their nobles and courtiers under control. The most important new laws were introduced by Prince Shotoku (AD574–622) and Prince Naka no Oe (AD626–671). Prince Naka considered his laws to be so important that he gave them the name *Taika* (Great Change). The Taika laws created a strong central government, run by a Grand Council of State, and a well-organized network of officials to oversee the 67 provinces.

DANCE
A Bugaku performer makes a slow, stately movement. Bugaku is an ancient form of dance that was popular at the emperor's court over 1,000 years ago. It is still performed today.

POLITE BEHAVIOR
A group of ladies watches an archery contest from behind a screen at the edge of a firing range. The behavior of courtiers was governed by rigid etiquette. Noble ladies had to follow especially strict rules. It was bad manners for them to show their faces in public. Whenever men were present, the ladies crouched behind a low curtain or a screen, or hid their faces behind their wide sleeves or their fans. When traveling, they concealed themselves behind curtains or sliding panels fitted to their ox-carts. They also often left one sleeve dangling outside.

THE SHELL GAME
You will need: fresh clams, water bowl, paintbrush, gold paint, white paint, black paint, red paint, green paint, water pot.

1 Ask an adult to boil the clams. Allow them to cool and then remove the insides. Wash the shells and leave them to dry. When dry, paint the shells gold.

2 Carefully pull each pair of shells apart. Now paint an identical design on to each of a pair of clam shells. Start by painting a white, round face.

3 Add features to the face. In the past, popular pictures, such as scenes from the *Tale of Genji,* were painted onto the shell pairs.

NOBLES AT COURT

Two nobles are shown here riding a splendid horse. Noblemen at the imperial court spent much of their time on government business. They also practiced their riding and fighting skills, took part in court ceremonies, and read and wrote poetry.

THE IMPERIAL COURT

Life at court was both elegant and refined. The buildings were exquisite and set in beautiful gardens. Paintings based on the writings of courtiers show some of the famous places they enjoyed visiting.

THE FUJIWARA CLAN

Fujiwara Teika (1162–1241) was a poet and a member of the Fujiwara clan. This influential family gained power at court by arranging the marriages of their daughters to young princes and emperors. Between AD724 and 1900, 54 of the 76 emperors of Japan had mothers who were related to the Fujiwara clan.

A LOOK INSIDE

This scroll-painting shows rooms inside the emperor's palace and groups of courtiers strolling in the gardens outside. Indoors, the rooms are divided up by silken blinds and the courtiers sit on mats and cushions.

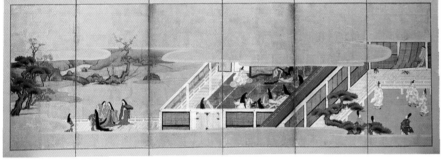

4 Paint several pairs of clam shells with various designs. Make sure that each pair of shells has an identical picture. Leave the painted shells to dry.

5 Turn all your shells face down and mix them up well. Turn over one shell then challenge your opponent to pick the matching shell to yours.

6 If the two shells do not match, turn them over and try again. If they do match, your opponent takes the shells. Take it in turns to challenge each other.

The person with the most shells wins! Noble ladies at the imperial court enjoyed playing the shell game. This is a simplified version of the game they used to play.

Japanese Military Power

I N 1159, a bloody civil war, known as the Heiji War, broke out in Japan between two powerful clans, the Taira and the Minamoto. The Taira were victorious in the Heiji War, and they controlled the government of the country for 26 years. However, the Minamoto rose again and regrouped to defeat the Taira in 1185.

Yoritomo, leader of the Minamoto clan, became the most powerful man in Japan and set up a new headquarters in the city of Kamakura. The emperor continued to act as head of the government in Kyoto, but he was effectively powerless. For almost the next 700 years, until 1868, military commanders such as Yoritomo, rather than the emperors, were the real rulers of Japan. They were known by the title *sei i tai shogun* (Great General Subduing the Barbarians).

SHOGUN FOR LIFE
Minamoto Yoritomo was the first person to take the title shogun and to hand the title on to his sons. In fact, the title did not stay in the Minamoto family for long because the family line died out in 1219. But new shogun families soon took its place.

FIRE! FIRE!
This scroll-painting illustrates the end of a siege during the Heiji War. The war was fought between two powerful clans, the Taira and the Minamoto. The rival armies set fire to buildings by shooting burning arrows and so drove the inhabitants out into the open where they could be killed.

MAKE A KITE
You will need: 31 in x 22 in card, ruler, pencil, dowels tapered at each end (5 x 20 in, 2 x 27½ in), masking tape, scissors, glue, brush, thread, paintbrush, paints, water pot, paper (21 in x 21 in), string, bamboo stick.

1 Draw a square 20 in x 20 in on card with a line down the centre. Lay the dowels on the square. Glue the dowels to each other and then tape.

2 When the glue has dried, remove the masking tape. Take the frame off the card. Bind the corners of the frame with the strong thread.

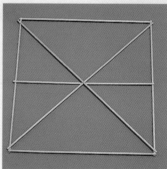

3 Now position your two longer dowels so that they cross in the middle of the square. Glue and then bind the corners with the strong thread.

DYNASTY FOUNDER

Tokugawa Ieyasu (1542-1616) was a noble from eastern Japan. He was one of three powerful warlords who brought long years of civil war to an end and unified Japan. In 1603 he won the battle of Sekigahara and became shogun. His family, the Tokugawa, ruled Japan for the next 267 years.

RESTING PLACE

This mausoleum (burial chamber) was built at Nikko in north-central Japan. It was created to house the body of the mighty shogun Tokugawa Ieyasu. Three times a year, Ieyasu's descendants traveled to Nikko to pay homage to their great ancestor.

UNDER ATTACK

Life in Nijo Castle, Kyoto, is shown in great detail on this painted screen. The castle belonged to the Tokugawa family of shoguns. Like emperors, great shoguns built themselves fine castles, which they used as centers of government or as fortresses in times of war. Nijo Castle was one of the finest buildings in Japan. It had "nightingale" floors that creaked loudly when an intruder stepped on them, raising the alarm. The noise was made to sound like a bird call.

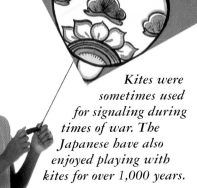

Kites were sometimes used for signaling during times of war. The Japanese have also enjoyed playing with kites for over 1,000 years.

4 Paint a colorful kite pattern on to the paper. It is a good idea to tape the edges of the paper down so it does not move around or curl up.

5 Draw light pencil marks ½ in in from the corners of the paper on all four sides. Carefully cut out the corners of the paper, as shown.

6 Glue the paper onto the kite frame. You will need to glue along the wooden frame and fold the paper over the edge of the frame. Leave to dry.

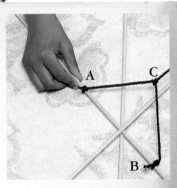

7 Tie a short length of string across the center of the kite frame (A to B). Knot a long kite string on to it as shown (C). Wind the string on the bamboo.

Imperial Life in Japan

IT WAS THE CUSTOM for each Japanese ruler to build a new palace when he or she came to power. But in AD710, the Empress Gemmei built a whole new city, at Nara. It became the government center for all Japan.

In AD794, Emperor Kammu decided to build a city that would be bigger and even more beautiful than Nara. He moved his imperial court to a new site, called Heian-kyo. Kammu based the plans for his new capital on the great Chinese city of Chang'an (modern Xian). The whole city was laid out as a rectangle, with main streets running at right angles to one another. The emperor's palace was in the north of the city, and courtiers lived in elegant *shinden* (single-story villas) close by. Workers and lower officials lived on the outskirts. Heian-kyo (modern Kyoto) was home to the Japanese emperors for over 1,000 years, until 1868 when Emperor Meiji came to power. Its royal and noble inhabitants became known as the people who lived in the clouds, because they lived shut away from ordinary, everyday life.

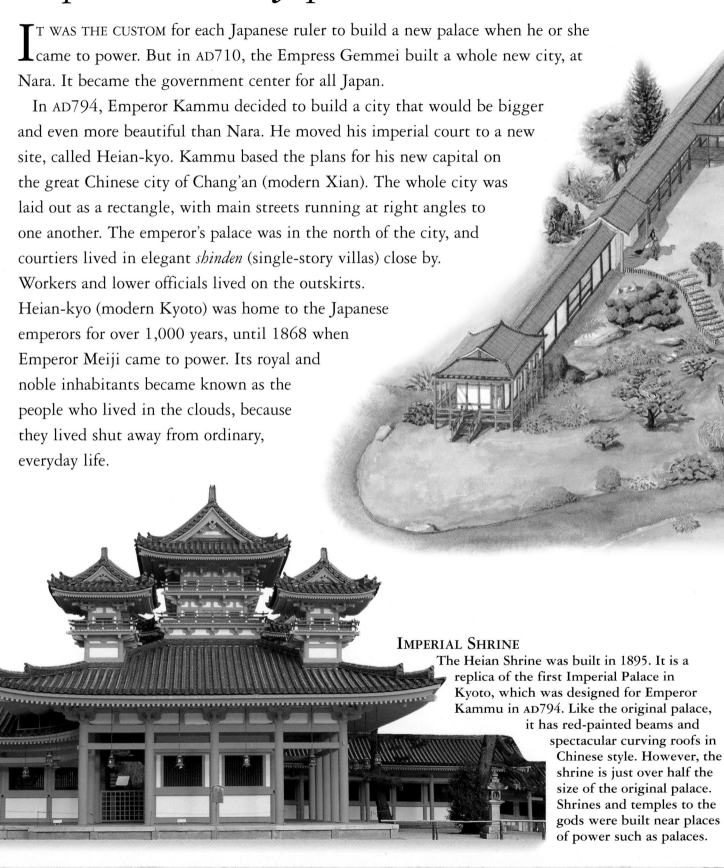

IMPERIAL SHRINE

The Heian Shrine was built in 1895. It is a replica of the first Imperial Palace in Kyoto, which was designed for Emperor Kammu in AD794. Like the original palace, it has red-painted beams and spectacular curving roofs in Chinese style. However, the shrine is just over half the size of the original palace. Shrines and temples to the gods were built near places of power such as palaces.

LIFE IN A *SHINDEN*

In *Heian-kyo*, nobles and courtiers lived in splendid *shinden* (houses) like this one. Each *shinden* was designed as a number of separate buildings, linked by covered walkways. It was usually set in a landscaped garden, with artificial hills, ornamental trees, bridges, pavilions and ponds. Sometimes a stream flowed through the garden – and through parts of the house, as well. The various members of the noble family, and their servants, lived in different parts of the *shinden*.

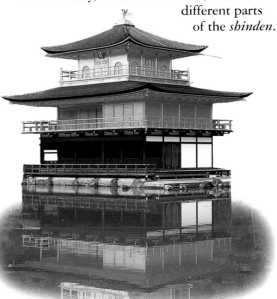

GOLDEN PAVILION

This is a replica of the Kinkakuji (Temple of the Golden Pavilion). The original was completed in 1397 and survived until 1950. But, like many of Kyoto's old wooden buildings, it was destroyed by fire. The walls of the pavilion are covered in gold leaf. The golden glow is reflected in the calm waters of a shallow lake.

SILVER TEMPLE

The Ginkakuji (Temple of the Silver Pavilion) in Kyoto was completed in 1483. Despite its name, it was never painted silver, but left as natural wood.

THRONE ROOM

The Shishinden Enthronement Hall is within the palace compound in Kyoto. The emperor would have sat on the raised platform (left) while his courtiers bowed low before him. This palace was the main residence for all emperors from 1331 to 1868.

Organized Government in Greece

ANCIENT GREECE WAS MADE UP of about 300 separate city states. Some were no bigger than villages, while others centered around cities such as Sparta or Athens. Each city state was known as a *polis* (from which we take our word politics) and had its own laws and government.

In the 4th century BC, the Greek philosopher Aristotle wrote that there were various types of government. Autocracy was power held by one person. This might be a monarch, on account of his royal birth, or a tyrant who had siezed power by force. Oligarchy was government by a few people. These might be aristocrats who assumed control by right of noble birth, or a group of rich and powerful people. Democratic government was rule by many and was only practiced in Athens. It gave every male citizen the right to vote, hold public office or serve on a jury. However, women, slaves and foreigners were not counted as full citizens.

SET IN STONE
The laws of the city of Ephesus were carved on stone tablets in both Greek and Latin. The Greeks believed that their laws had to be clearly set in stone and seen by everyone if all citizens were to be expected to obey them.

BEHIND THE SCENES
Women were not allowed to take an active part in politics in ancient Greece. However, some played an important role behind the scenes. One such woman was Aspasia, a professional entertainer. She met and became mistress to Pericles, one of the most influential Athenian statesmen of the 5th century BC. Pericles confided in his mistress about affairs of state. He came to rely on her insight and wisdom in his judgment of people and situations.

VOTING TOKENS
You will need: pair of compasses, thin card, pencil, ruler, scissors, rolling pin, cutting board, self-hardening clay, modeling tool, balsa wood stick 2 in long, piece of drinking straw 2 in long, bronze-colored paint, paintbrush, water pot.

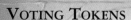

1 Make two templates. Use a pair of compasses to draw two circles, on a piece of thin card. Make each one 1½ in in diameter. Cut them out.

2 Use a rolling pin to roll out the clay to 1 in thickness. Use a modeling tool to cut around the card circles into the clay. Press down hard as you do this.

3 Make a hole in the center of each clay circle. Use the balsa wood to make one hole (innocent token). Use the straw to make the other hole (guilty token).

People Power

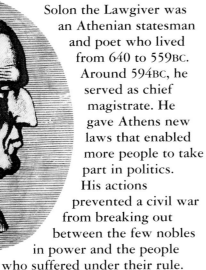

Solon the Lawgiver was an Athenian statesman and poet who lived from 640 to 559BC. Around 594BC, he served as chief magistrate. He gave Athens new laws that enabled more people to take part in politics. His actions prevented a civil war from breaking out between the few nobles in power and the people who suffered under their rule.

Vote Here

This terracotta urn was used to collect voting tokens. They were used in Athens when votes needed to be taken in law courts or when the voters' intentions needed to be kept secret. Each voter put a bronze disk in the urn to register his decision. Normally, voting was done by a show of hands, which was difficult to count precisely.

Face to Face

The ruins of this council chamber at Priene in present-day Turkey show how seating was arranged. The tiered, three-sided square enabled each councilor to see and hear clearly all of the speakers involved in a debate. Even in the democracies of ancient Greece, most everyday decisions were taken by committees or councils and not by the assembly of voters.

4 Write a name on the innocent token using the modeling tool. Carefully push the balsa stick through the hole. Leave it to dry.

5 Write another name on the guilty token using the modeling tool. Carefully push the drinking straw through the hole. Leave it to dry.

6 Wait until the clay tokens are dry before painting them. The original tokens were made from bronze, so use a bronze-colored paint.

Jurors were issued with two tokens to vote with. A hollow center meant that the juror thought the accused was guilty. A solid center meant that the juror thought the accused was innocent.

Inequality in Greece

GREEK SOCIETY WAS DIVIDED by a strict social structure that was enforced by its governments. Most city states were ruled by a small group of people (oligarchy). Two exceptions were the powerful cities of Sparta and Athens. Sparta held on to its monarchy, while Athens introduced the first democratic government in history. In the city of Athens, all citizens could vote and hold office. However to be a citizen, it was necessary to be an adult male, born in the city itself. Even so-called democratic Athens was ruled by a minority of the people who lived there. The treatment of *metics* (foreign residents), women, slaves and children was just the same as in other city states.

Women had no legal rights and rarely took part in public life. Metics had to pay extra taxes and serve in the army, but could not own land or marry an Athenian. The Athenians felt uneasy about the large number of metics living in their city, but depended upon their skills.

Slaves made up half the population of Athens. Most of them had been born to slaves, were prisoners of war or captives of pirates. Even native Greeks could become slaves by falling into debt, but they were freed once the debt was paid off.

WARRIORS AND WEALTH
Only the wealthiest members of society could afford to arm themselves for war. Bronze weapons were expensive. In early centuries, the poor were given supporting jobs, such as slingers or carriers of supplies. However, as cities grew richer, weapons were manufactured at public expense by slaves, and most male citizens were expected to carry arms.

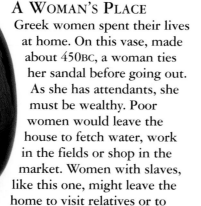

A WOMAN'S PLACE
Greek women spent their lives at home. On this vase, made about 450BC, a woman ties her sandal before going out. As she has attendants, she must be wealthy. Poor women would leave the house to fetch water, work in the fields or shop in the market. Women with slaves, like this one, might leave the home to visit relatives or to pray at a shrine or temple.

LOVED ONES
A young girl and her pet dog are seen on this tombstone from the 4th century BC. The likely expense of such a detailed carving suggests that she was dearly loved. Not all children were cherished. Girl babies, and sick babies of either sex, were often left outside to die. Some were underfed and fell victim to diseases. Greek law required children to support their parents in old age. Childless couples were always keen to adopt, and sometimes rescued abandoned children.

CRAFTSMAN

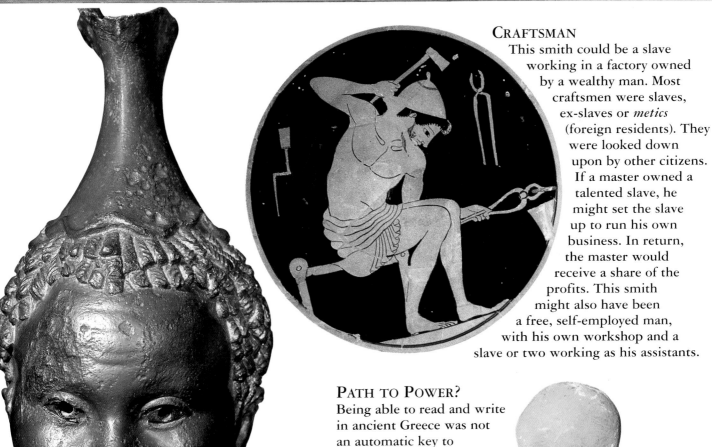

This smith could be a slave working in a factory owned by a wealthy man. Most craftsmen were slaves, ex-slaves or *metics* (foreign residents). They were looked down upon by other citizens. If a master owned a talented slave, he might set the slave up to run his own business. In return, the master would receive a share of the profits. This smith might also have been a free, self-employed man, with his own workshop and a slave or two working as his assistants.

PATH TO POWER?

Being able to read and write in ancient Greece was not an automatic key to success. The Greek alphabet could be learned quite easily. Even slaves could become highly educated scribes. However, illiterate men were unlikely to hold high positions, except perhaps in Sparta, where written records were rarely kept. Although women were denied the right to a formal education, they were often able to read and write enough to keep a record of household stores.

ENSLAVED BY LANGUAGE

This Roman bottle is made in the shape of an African slave girl's head. The Greeks also owned slaves. The Greek philosopher Aristotle argued that some people were "naturally" meant to be slaves. His opinion was shared by many of his countrymen. He felt that this applied most obviously to people who did not speak Greek. Slaves were treated with varying degrees of kindness and hostility. Some were worked to death by their owners, but others had good jobs as clerks or bailiffs. A few hundred slaves were owned by the city of Athens and served as policemen, coin-inspectors and clerks of the court.

Rulers of Rome

IN ITS EARLY DAYS, the city of Rome was ruled by kings. The first king was said to be Romulus, the founder of the city in 753BC. The last king, a hated tyrant called Tarquinius the Proud, was thrown out in 509BC. The Romans then set up a republic. The Senate, an assembly of powerful and wealthy citizens, chose two consuls to lead them each year. By 493BC, the common people had their own representatives – the tribunes – to defend their rights in the Senate. In times of crisis, rulers could take on emergency powers and become dictators. The first Roman emperor, Augustus, was appointed by the Senate in 27BC. The emperors were given great powers and were even worshipped as gods. Some lived simply and ruled well, but others were violent and cruel. They were surrounded by flatterers, and yet were in constant fear of their lives.

TRIUMPHAL PROCESSION
When a Roman general won a great victory, he was honored with a military parade called a triumph. Cheering crowds lined the streets as the grand procession passed by. If a general was successful and popular, the way to power was often open to him. Probably the most famous Roman ruler of all, Julius Caesar, came to power after a series of brilliant military conquests.

STATE SACRIFICE
Roman emperors had religious as well as political duties. As *pontifex maximus*, or high priest, an emperor would make sacrifices as offerings to the gods at important festivals.

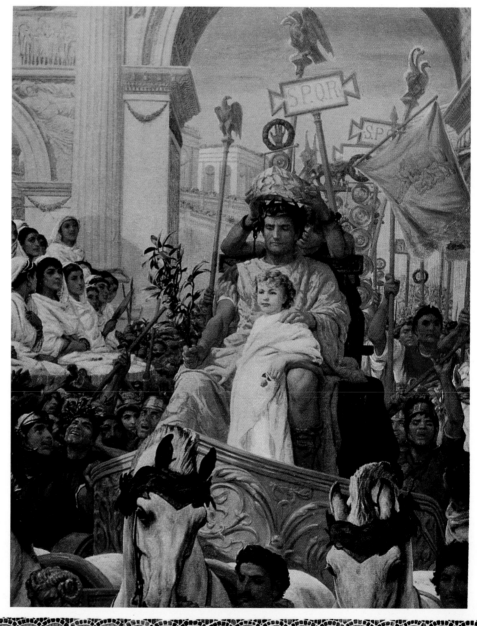

figs

DEADLY FRUIT

Who killed Augustus, the first Roman emperor, in AD14? It was hard to say. It might have been a natural death... but then again, it might have been caused by his wife Livia. She was said to have coated the figs in his garden with a deadly poison. Roman emperors were much feared, but they were surrounded by enemies and could trust no one, least of all their own families.

GUARDING THE EMPEROR

The Praetorian Guards were the emperor's personal bodyguards. They wore special uniforms, were well paid and they were the only armed soldiers allowed in the city of Rome. They became very powerful and sometimes took power into their own hands. Guards assassinated the emperor Caligula and elected Claudius to succeed him.

In Rome, wreaths made from leaves of the laurel tree were worn by emperors, victorious soldiers and athletes. The wreath was a badge of honor. The Romans copied the idea from the ancient Greeks.

WREATH OF HONOR

You will need: tape measure, garden wire, pliers, scissors, Scotch tape, green ribbon, bay or laurel leaves (real or fake).

1 Measure around your head with the tape measure. Cut some wire the same length, so the wreath will fit you. Bend the wire as shown and tape the ribbon around it.

2 Start to tape the leaves by their stems onto the wire, as shown above. Work your way around to the middle of the wire, fanning out the leaves as you go.

3 Then reverse the direction of the leaves and work your way around the rest of the wire. Fit the finished wreath to your head. Hail, Caesar!

Masters and Slaves in Rome

ROMAN SOCIETY was never very fair. In the early days of the Republic, a group of rich and powerful noble families, called the patricians, controlled the city and the Senate. A citizen who wanted his voice heard had to persuade a senator to speak on his behalf. Over the centuries the common citizens, known as plebeians, became more powerful. By 287BC, they shared equally in government. Eventually, in the days of the Empire, even people of humble birth could become emperor, provided they were wealthy or had the support of the army. Emperors always feared riots by the common people of Rome, so they tried to keep the people happy with handouts of free food and lavish entertainments. Roman women could not vote. Most had little power outside the family, but some were successful in business or influenced political events through their husbands. Slaves had very few rights, even though Roman society was dependent on their labor. Prisoners of war were sold as slaves, Many were treated cruelly and revolts were common.

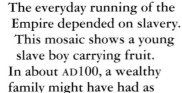

A ROMAN CONSUL
This is a statue of a Roman consul, or leader of the Senate, in the days of the Republic. At first, only members of the noble and wealthy class could be senators. However, under the emperors, the power and influence of the Senate slowly grew less.

LIFE AS A SLAVE
The everyday running of the Empire depended on slavery. This mosaic shows a young slave boy carrying fruit. In about AD100, a wealthy family might have had as many as 500 slaves. Some families treated their slaves well, and slaves who gave good service might earn their freedom. However, many more led miserable lives, toiling in the mines or laboring in the fields.

SLAVE TAG
This bronze disc was probably worn like a dog tag around the neck of a slave. The Latin words on it say: "Hold me, in case I run away, and return me to my master Viventius on the estate of Callistus." Slaves had few rights and could be branded on the forehead or leg as the property of their owners.

COLLECTING TAXES

This stone carving probably shows people paying their annual taxes. Officials counted the population of the Empire and registered them for paying tax. Money from taxes paid for the army and running the government. However, many of the tax collectors took bribes, and even emperors seized public money to add to their private fortunes.

ARISTOCRATS

This Italian painting of the 1700s imagines how a noble Roman lady might dress after bathing. Wealthy people had personal slaves to help them bathe, dress and look after their hair. Household slaves were sometimes almost part of the family, and their children might be brought up and educated with their owner's children.

Celtic Societies

THE CELTS WERE NEVER a single, unified nation. Instead there were many separate tribes throughout Europe. Greek and Roman writers recorded many Celtic tribal names, for example, the Helvetii (who lived in Switzerland) and the Caledones (who lived in Scotland). Tribes sometimes made friendly alliances with one another, or with a stronger power such as Rome. This usually happened when a tribe was threatened by invaders or at war. Within each tribe, there were many clans. These were families who traced their descent from a single ancestor, and who shared ties of loyalty and a family name.

Each tribe was headed by a king (or chieftain). His task was to lead men in battle and on raids, and to maintain peace and prosperity. Kings were chosen from rich noble families. Senior noblemen were expected to support the king and to lead their own bands of warriors. Druids (Celtic priests) and bards (well-educated poets) also came from noble families. Farmers and craftworkers ranked lower, but they were highly valued for their important skills. There were also servants and slaves.

GUARDIAN GODDESS
Many Celtic tribes had their own special god or goddess, to protect them and to bring fertility to their farm animals and crops. This mother goddess was the special guardian of a Celtic tribe who lived in Austria. She is shown gently cradling twin babies, looking after them with her magical protective powers. After a battle, the Celts sacrificed a share of all they had captured to their favorite gods and goddesses.

PROUD LEADER
This stone statue of a Celtic king or chieftain from Gaul (modern France) was made around 50 BC. He is dressed ready to lead his tribe into war, in a chain-mail tunic and a magic torc. His torc (neck ornament) is an indication of high rank, but we have no idea who he actually was.

Religious support, knowledge, rituals

Protection and offerings

Gifts and prestige

Loyalty and help in battle

Chieftains

Protection and offerings

Religious support

Farmers and craftworkers

Druids and bards

Nobles and warriors

Religious support

Respect and offerings

Respect and manpower

Protection and access to land

THE STRUCTURE OF SOCIETY

All the different groups within Celtic society had an important part to play. They relied on one another to survive. This diagram shows what each different group gave to society, and what it received in return. Chieftains offered leadership and inspired loyalty. Nobles and warriors protected the tribe from attack. Farmers and craftworkers produced food and goods. Druids and bards provided religious support and celebrated tribal pride. The lowest social rank was held by laborers and slaves. They did jobs that were often hard and dirty.

TRIBAL COIN

Many Celtic tribes issued coins, marked with their own special design. This coin was made for the Catuvellauni tribe who lived in southern England. It shows a warrior on horseback riding into battle brandishing a carnyx (war-trumpet). It was designed to tell everyone what a brave and warlike people the Catuvellauni were.

SLAVE CHAIN

Chains like these were used to stop slaves running away. The round iron bracelets, joined by links of heavy metal, were fastened around a slave's wrists or ankles and locked shut. Slavery was never very important in Celtic society. There were many more free people than slaves. However, slaves were used for dirty, difficult, dangerous work (for example, in the salt mines at Hallstatt, Germany).

Viking Rulers and Freemen

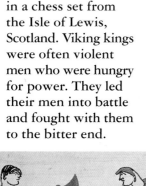

STRONG RULERS
This king is a piece in a chess set from the Isle of Lewis, Scotland. Viking kings were often violent men who were hungry for power. They led their men into battle and fought with them to the bitter end.

MOST VIKINGS WERE KARLS (freemen) who owned some land and a farm, and went to sea for raids and adventures. Other karls were merchants, ship builders or craft workers. The free Vikings used *thralls* (slaves) as laborers and servants on farms and in workshops. Many Vikings were slave-traders. Prisoners who had been captured on raids all over Europe were sold as thralls. Viking society allowed thralls few rights. Their children were slaves as well.

The most powerful and wealthy Vikings were chieftains or *jarls* (earls). They controlled large areas in Norway and Sweden, and some jarls became local kings. Viking kings became more powerful as they conquered new lands and united them into kingdoms. By 900, Harald Finehair, King of Vestfold, had brought all of Norway under his control. Denmark had always been ruled by a single person, and in the reign of Harald Bluetooth, government became even more centralized. Yet the early Vikings had been quarrelsome and proud people, who bridled against any centralized control. This remained true in colonies such as

Iceland. Many people, including Eric the Red, fled to Iceland to escape the law, or because they did not want to be ruled by a distant king. Iceland remained an independent republic throughout the Viking Age. However, after 1100, it was forced to recognize a Norwegian king.

FIGHTING FORCE
Karls (freemen), formed the backbone of a Scandinavian invasion force when the Normans attacked England in 1066. This scene is part of the Bayeux tapestry and shows Norman karls preparing for conquest.

FARMERS
Viking karls (freemen) built farmhouses on the Shetland islands to the north of Scotland. The search for new land to farm led many karls to travel overseas. The buildings on Shetland were made of timber, stone and turf. This Viking site is known as Jarlshof today.

LOYAL TO YOUR LORD

This reconstruction of a Viking raid is taking place on the island of Lindisfarne in northern England. Viking raiders first attacked Lindisfarne in the year 793. A typical war band would have been made up of karls (freemen). In battle, they followed their jarl (earl), into the thick of the fighting without hesitation. They formed a tight guard around him when the fighting got tough. In the early Viking days, it was more important to show loyalty to one's family or lord than to a kingdom.

DEFENSIVE FORT

King Harald Bluetooth had a series of forts built to defend the Danish kingdom in the 980s. This one is at Fyrkat, in Jutland. By the end of the Viking period, it was very rare for independent Viking chieftains to lead small bands of karls on raids.

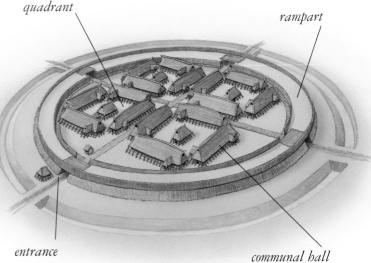

quadrant

rampart

entrance

communal hall

A RESTLESS PEOPLE

Poor farmhands prepare wool in this reconstruction showing Vikings at work. Families of all social classes left Scandinavia to settle new lands during the Viking age. They were driven by the need for land and wealth. They faced long sea voyages and years of hard work building new farms or towns.

Viking Assemblies

EACH REGION AND LAND where the Vikings settled had its own public assembly called the *Thing*, where laws and judgments were passed. The Thing met at regular intervals and was made up only of karls (freemen). Women and slaves had no right to speak there.

The Thing had great powers, and it could even decide who should be king. If someone was murdered or robbed, the victim's relatives could go to the Thing and demand justice. Everybody in the assembly considered the case. If they all agreed that a person was guilty, then judgment was passed. The person sentenced might have to pay a fine of money or other valuable goods. Sometimes the only way a dispute could be settled was by mortal combat (a fight to the death). However, mortal combat was made illegal in Iceland and Norway around AD1000. The assembly also dealt with arguments over property, marriage and divorce.

In Iceland there was no king at all in the Viking period. Instead, an *Althing* or national assembly was held each midsummer. The Althing was a cross between a court, a parliament and a festival. It was a chance for families to come in from their isolated farmhouses and meet up with each other. The assembly approved laws that had been drafted by the jarls and elected a Law Speaker.

PAY UP
The Thing could order a criminal to pay the victim, in the form of money or goods. If the criminal failed to do so, he was made an outlaw. This entitled anyone to kill him.

MEETING PLACE
The Icelandic Althing met on the Thingvellir, a rocky plain east of the city of Reykjavik. A Law Speaker read out the laws, which had been passed by a group of 39 chieftains, from the Law Rock. The Althing is the world's oldest surviving law-making assembly on record. It met from 930 until 1800 and again from 1843. Today it is Iceland's parliament.

A DIFFICULT DECISION

This carving shows an important gathering of the Althing in 1000. The assembly was split over a difficult decision – should Iceland become Christian? It was left to the Law Speaker to decide. After a lot of thought, he ruled that the country should be officially Christian, but that people who wished to worship the old gods could do so in private.

MANX LAW

An earth mound marks the site of the old Viking assembly on the Isle of Man. The Vikings who settled on the island, off the west coast of Great Britain, called this assembly field the Tynwald. This is also the name of the island's parliament today. The Tynwald still has the power to make the island's laws.

MORTAL COMBAT

A Viking duel is reenacted today. Life was cheap in Viking times, and violent death was common. A fight to the death was an official way of settling a serious dispute, such as an accusation of murder. This system of justice was taken to England by the Normans in 1066.

LAW MAKERS

Viking chieftains would ride to Iceland's Thingvellir (Assembly Plain) from all over the island. This 19th-century painting by W.G. Collingwood shows chieftains gathering for the Althing. This assembly was held only once a year.

Aztec and Maya Social Order

THE NECK OF LAND BETWEEN North and South America, that is known as Mesoamerica, was never a single, united country. During the Maya (AD250-900) and later Aztec civilizations, it was divided into several, separate states. The rulers of these states often combined the roles of army commanders, law-makers and priests. Some claimed to be descended from the gods. Rulers were almost always men. Mesoamerican women – especially among the Maya – had important religious duties but rarely took part in law-making or army life. Maya rulers were called *ahaw* (lord) or *mahk'ina* (great Sun lord), and each city-state had its own royal family.

The supreme Aztec leader was called the *tlatoani* (speaker). Originally, he was elected from army commanders by the Aztec people. Later, he was chosen from the family of the previous leader. He ruled all Aztec lands, helped by a deputy called *cihuacoatl* (snake woman), nobles and army commanders. Rulers, priests and nobles made up a tiny part of society. Ordinary citizens were called *macehualtin*. Men were farmers, fishermen or craftworkers. There were thousands of slaves, who were criminals, enemy captives or poor people who had given up their freedom in return for food and shelter.

OFFICIAL HELP
This Maya clay figure shows a scribe at work. Well-trained officials, such as scribes, helped Mesoamerican rulers by keeping careful records. Scribes also painted ceremonial pottery.

HONOR TO THE KING
Painted pottery vases like this were buried alongside powerful Maya people. They show scenes from legends and royal palace life. Here, a lord presents tribute to the king.

MAYA NOBLEWOMAN
This terracotta figure of a Maya noblewoman dates from between AD600 and 900. She is richly attired and is protecting her face with a parasol. Women did not usually hold official positions in Mesoamerican lands. Instead queens and other noblewomen influenced their husbands by offering tactful suggestions and wise advice. Whether she was rich or poor, a woman's main duty was to provide children for her husband and to support him in all aspects of his work.

THE RULING CLASS

A noble is shown getting ready for a ceremony in this Aztec picture. Aztec nobles played an important part in government. They were chosen by rulers to be judges, army commanders and officials. Nobles with government jobs paid no taxes and were given a free house to live in. Noble men and women came from ancient families who were related to the rulers. It was, however, possible for an ordinary man to achieve higher rank if he fought very bravely in battle and captured four enemy soldiers alive.

WAR LEADER

A Maya stone carving shows ruler Shield Jaguar (below left) getting ready to lead his army in AD724. He is wearing a padded tunic and holding a knife in his right hand. His wife, Lady Xoc, is handing him his jaguar headdress. Maya rulers also took part in religious ceremonies, where they offered drops of their blood to the gods in return for their help.

MEN AT WORK

Aztec farmers are harvesting ripe cobs of corn. This painting comes from the Florentine Codex. This 12-volume manuscript was made by a Spanish friar. Codex pictures like this tell us a lot about ordinary peoples' everyday lives. Notice how simply the farmers are dressed compared to the more powerful people on these pages.

Life at the Top in Mesoamerica

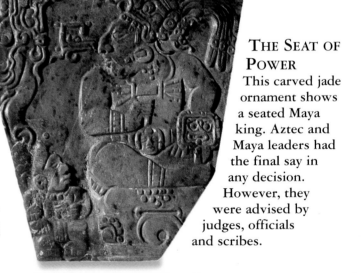

The RULERS OF EACH Maya and Aztec city-state lived in splendid palaces that were a reflection of their power and wealth. The palace of the Aztec ruler Moctezuma II in Tenochtitlan was vast. It had banqueting rooms big enough to seat 3,000 guests, private apartments, a library, a schoolroom, kitchens, stores, an arsenal for weapons, separate women's quarters, spectacular gardens and a large zoo. Etiquette around the emperor was very strict. Captains of the royal bodyguard had to approach Moctezuma barefoot, with downcast eyes, making low bows and murmuring, "Lord, my lord, my great lord." When they left, they had to walk backward, keeping their gaze away from his face.

Palaces were also the government headquarters where rulers greeted ambassadors from neighboring city-states and talked with advisors.

Rulers had the power to make strict laws. Each city-state had its own law-courts, where formidable judges had the power of life and death.

ROYAL RECORD
Maya rulers set up stelae (stone pillars) in their cities. Carved pictures recorded major people and events of their reigns. This one celebrates a Maya ruler in Copan, Honduras.

THE SEAT OF POWER
This carved jade ornament shows a seated Maya king. Aztec and Maya leaders had the final say in any decision. However, they were advised by judges, officials and scribes.

MAKE A FEATHER FAN

You will need: pencil, thick card, scissors, thin red card, green paper, double-sided tape, feathers (real or paper), masking tape, paints, paintbrushes, colored felt, Elmer's glue and brush, Scotch tape, colored wool, bamboo cane.

1 Draw two rings about 1½ ft in diameter and 3 in wide on thick card. Cut them out. Make another ring the same size from thin red card, as above.

2 Cut lots of leaf shapes from green paper. Stick them around the edge of one thick card ring using double-sided tape. Add some real or paper feathers.

3 Cut two circles about 4½ in in diameter from thin red card. Draw around something the right size, such as a reel of tape. These are for the center of the fan.

LOCKED UP

A group of Aztec judges discusses how best to punish prisoners in the cage. Punishments were very severe. If ordinary citizens broke the law, they might be beaten or speared with cactus spines. For a second offense, they might be stoned to death.

FIT FOR A KING

An Aztec picture shows visitors at a ruler's palace. Spanish explorers in the 1500s reported that over 600 nobles visited the Aztec ruler's palace every day. They attended council meetings, consulted palace officials, asked favors from the ruler and made their views heard. It was the Aztec tradition that the ruler sat on a mat on the floor with his council.

THE RULE OF THE GODS

In this stone carving, a human face is being swallowed by a magic serpent. Royal and government buildings were often decorated with carvings like this. They signified the religious power of the ruler of a particular city.

Beautiful feather fans rather like this were used by Aztec nobles and rulers to keep themselves cool.

4 Paint a flower on one of the two smaller red circles and a butterfly on the other. Cut v-shapes from the felt and glue them to the large red ring.

5 Using sticky tape, fix lengths of colored wool to the back of one of the red circles, as shown. Place the red circle in the center of the ring with leaves.

6 Tape the lengths of wool to the outer ring to look like spokes. Coat the ring with Elmer's glue and place the second card ring on top, putting a cane in between.

7 Use double-sided tape to stick the second red circle face up in the center. Glue the red ring with felt v-shapes on top of the second thick card ring.

Inca Lords of the Sun

THE INCAS WERE ORIGINALLY a tribal people of the Peruvian Andes in the 1100s. As the tribes grew in size, strong leaders began to take control. Under them, the Incas began to conquer neighboring lands in the 1300s. During the 1400s, the mighty Inca Empire had developed.

The Inca emperor was called *Sapa Inca* (Only Leader). He was regarded as a god, a descendant of the Sun. He had complete power over his subjects, and was treated with the utmost respect at all times, but was always on his guard. There were many rivals for the throne among his royal relations. Each emperor had a new palace built for himself in the royal city of Cuzco. Emperors were often veiled or screened from ordinary people.

The empress, or *Quya* (Star), was the emperor's sister or mother. She was also thought to be divine and led the worship of the Moon goddess. The next emperor was supposed to be chosen from among her sons. An emperor had many secondary wives. Waskar was said to have fathered eighty children in just eight years.

RELIGIOUS LEADERS

Sacrifices of llamas were made to the gods each month, at special festivals and before battle. The *Sapa Inca* controlled all religious activities. In the 1400s, the emperor Wiraqocha Inka declared that worship of the god Wiraqocha, the Creator (after whom he was named), was more important than worship of Inti, the Sun god. This made some people angry.

A CHOSEN WOMAN

Figurines of young girls were originally dressed, but the specially made clothes have perished or been lost over the years. Chosen girls (*akllakuna*), were educated for four years in religion, weaving and housekeeping. Some became the emperor's secondary wives or married noblemen. Others became priestesses or *mamakuna* (virgins of the Sun).

MAKE AN EMPEROR'S FAN

You will need: pencil, card, ruler, scissors, paints in bright colors, paintbrush, water pot, masking tape, wadding, Elmer's glue, hessian or sackcloth, needle, thread, string or twine.

1 Draw a feather shape 7 in long on to card and cut it out. The narrow part should be half of this length. Draw around the shape on card nine times.

2 Carefully paint the feathers with bright colors. Use red, orange and yellow to look like rain-forest birds. Allow the paint to dry completely.

3 Cut out each feather and snip along the sides of the widest part to give a feathery effect. When the paint is dry, paint the other side as well.

COMMANDER IN CHIEF

The emperor sits on his throne. He wears a tasselled woolen headdress or *llautu*, decorated with gold and feathers, and large gold earplugs. He carries a scepter. Around him, army chiefs await their orders. Emperors played an active part in military campaigns and relied on the army to keep them in power.

COOL SPRINGS

At Tambo Machay, to the south of Cuzco, fresh, cold water is channeled from sacred springs. Here, the great Pachakuti Inka Yupanki would bathe after a hard day's hunting.

THE LIVING DEAD

The dead body of an emperor, preserved as a mummy, is paraded through the streets. When each emperor died, his palace became his tomb. Once a year, the body was carried around Cuzco amid great celebrations. The picture is by Guamán Poma de Ayala, who was of Inca descent. In the 1600s, he made many pictures of Inca life.

Feathers from birds of the tropical forests to the east of the Andes were used to make fans for the emperor.

4 Hold the narrow ends of the feathers and spread out the tops to form a fan shape. Use masking tape to secure the ends firmly in position.

5 Cut a rectangular piece of wadding 3½ in high and long enough to wrap the base of the feathers several times. Use glue on one side to keep it in place.

6 Cut a strip of hessian or sackcloth about 2 in wide. Starting at the base of the feathers, wrap the fabric around the stems. Hold it in place with a few stitches.

7 Wind string or twine firmly around the hessian to form the fan's handle. Tuck in the ends and use glue at each end to make sure they are secure.

Controlling Inca Society

FAMILY CONNECTIONS PLAYED an important part in royal power struggles and in everyday social organization in the Inca world. The nobles were grouped into family-based corporations called *panakas*. Members of each *panaka* shared rights to an area of land, its water, pasture and herds. Linked to each *panaka* was a land-holding *ayllu* (or clan) – a group of common people who were also related to each other.

The Incas managed to control an empire that contained many different peoples. Loyal Incas were sent to live in remote areas, while troublemakers from the regions were resettled nearer Cuzco, where they could be carefully watched. Conquered chiefs were called *kurakas*. They and their children were educated in Inca ways and allowed to keep some of their local powers.

The Inca system of law was quite severe. State officials and *kurakas* (conquered chiefs) acted as judges. Those who stole from the emperor's stores of grain, textiles and other goods faced a death sentence. Torture, beating, blinding and exile were all common punishments. The age of the criminal and the reason for the crime were sometimes taken into account.

A CLEVER CALCULATOR

One secret of Inca success was the *quipu*. It was used by government officials for recording all kinds of information, from the number of households in a town to the amount of goods of various kinds in a warehouse. The *quipu* was a series of strings tied to a thick cord. Each string had one or more colors and could be knotted. The colors represented anything from types of grain to groups of people. The knots represented numbers.

ONE STATE, MANY PEOPLES

The ancestors of these Bolivian women were subjects of the Incas. The Inca Empire was the largest ever known in all the Americas. It included at least a hundred different peoples. The Incas were clever governors and did not always try to force their own ideas upon other groups. Conquered peoples had to accept the Inca gods, but they were allowed to worship in their own way and keep their own customs.

A ROYAL INSPECTION

The Inca emperor Topa Inka Yupanki inspects government stores in the 1470s. In the Inca world, nearly all grain, textiles and other goods were produced for the State and stored in warehouses. Some extra produce might be bartered, or exchanged privately, but there were no big markets or stores.

PUBLIC WORKS

Laborers build fortifications on the borders of the Inca Empire. People paid their taxes to the Inca State in the form of labor called *mit'a*. This might be general work on the land. Men were also conscripted to work on public buildings or serve in the army. The Spanish continued to operate the *mit'a* as a form of tax long after they conquered the Inca Empire.

OLLANTAYTAMBO

This building in Ollantaytambo, in the Urubamba Valley, was once a State storehouse for the farm produce of the region. Ollantaytambo was a large town, which was probably built about 550 years ago. It protected the valley from raids by the warriors who lived in the forests to the east. Buildings dating from the Inca Empire were still being lived in by local people when the American archaeologist Dr Hiram Bingham passed through in 1911.

Levels of Inca Society

INCA SOCIETY was strictly graded. At the top were the *Sapa Inca* and his *Quya*. The High Priest and other important officials were normally recruited from members of the royal family.

If noblemen were loyal to the emperor, they might receive gifts of land. They might be given gold or a beautful *akllakuna* as a wife. They could expect jobs as regional governors, generals or priests. Lords and ladies wore fine clothes and were carried in splendid chairs, called litters.

Next in rank were the conquered non-Inca rulers and chiefs, the *kurakas*. They were cleverly brought into the Inca political system and given traditional honors. They served as regional judges.

Most people in the Empire were peasants. They were unable to leave their villages without official permission. They had no choice but to stay and toil on the land, sending their produce to the government stores.

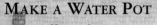

A TRUE NOBLEMAN
This man's headdress sets him apart as a noble or possibly a high priest. The model dates from a pre-Inca civilization 1,500-2,000 years ago. The Incas absorbed many different cultures into their own civilization.

CRAFT AND CLASS
A pottery figure from the Peruvian coast shows a porter carrying a water pot on his back. In the Inca Empire, craft workers such as potters and goldsmiths were employed by the State. They formed a small middle class. Unlike peasants they were never made to do *mit'a* (public service).

MAKE A WATER POT
You will need: self-drying clay, cutting board, rolling pin, ruler, water, water pot, acrylic paints, paintbrush.

1 Roll out a piece of clay on the board. Make a circle about 6½ in in diameter and ½ in thick. This will form the base of your water pot.

2 Roll some more clay into long sausages, about as fat as your little finger. Dampen the base with water and carefully place a sausage around the edge.

3 Coil more clay sausages on top of each other to build up the pot. Make each coil slightly smaller than the one below. Water will help them stick.

A PEASANT'S LIFE

A woman harvests potatoes near Sicuani, to the south of Cuzco. Then, as now, life was hard for the peasant farmers of the Andes. Both men and women worked in the fields, and even young children and the elderly were expected to help. However, the Inca State did provide some support for the peasants, supplying free grain in times of famine.

PLUGGED IN

Earplugs like this one, made of gold, turquoise and shell, were worn as a badge of rank. Inca noblemen wore such heavy gold earplugs that the Spanish called them *orejones* (big ears). Noblewomen wore their hair long, covered with a head-cloth.

LAND AND SEASONS

One third of all land and produce belonged to the emperor, one third to the priests and one third to the peasants. It was hardly a fair division. A peasant's life, digging, planting and harvesting, was ruled by the seasons. Each new season was celebrated by religious festivals and ceremonies.

Children were expected to help their parents by fetching water from the wells and mountain springs.

4 When you reach the neck of the pot, start making the coils slightly bigger again to form a lip. Carefully smooth the coils with wet fingertips.

5 Use two more rolls of clay to make handles on opposite sides of the pot. Smooth out the joints carefully to make sure the handles stay in place.

6 Leave the clay to dry completely. Then paint the pot all over with a background color. Choose an earthy reddish brown to look like Inca pottery.

7 Leave the reddish brown color to dry. Use a fine paintbrush and black paint to draw Inca designs on the pot like the ones in the picture above.

Tribes in North America

FROM AROUND 3000BC, many different tribal societies developed throughout North America, from the Apaches in the South to the Inuits of the far North. A single tribe might be as small as ten families or number thousands. Tribes came together in times of war, for ceremonies and for trading, or to form powerful confederacies (unions). Some Algonquin people formed the Powhatan Confederacy and controlled the coast of present-day Virginia. In the South-east, the Creek, Seminole, Cherokee, Choctaw and Chickasaw were known by Europeans as the "Five Civilized Tribes" because their system of law courts and land rights developed from European influences.

MAGNIFICENTLY COSTUMED
American Horse of the Oglala Sioux wears a double-trail war bonnet. His painted shirt shows he was a member of the Ogle Tanka'un or Shirt Wearers, who were wise and brave.

COMMITTEE MEETING
A Sioux council gathers to hear the head chief speak. Councils were made up of several leaders or chiefs. They elected the head chief whose authority came from his knowledge of tribal lore and skill as a warrior.

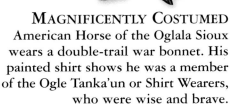

MAKE A SKIN ROBE

You will need: an old single sheet (or large piece of thin cotton fabric), scissors, tape measure or ruler, pencil, large needle, brown thread, felt in red, yellow, dark blue and light blue, Elmer's glue, glue brush, black embroidery thread (or string), red cotton thread (or other color).

1 Take the sheet and cut out a rectangle 4 ft, 7 in x 2 ft. Then cut out two 16 in x 13½ in rectangles for the arms. Fold the main (body) piece in half.

2 At the center of fold, draw a neckline 8¾ in across and 2½ in deep. Cut it out. Roll fabric over at shoulders and stitch down with an overlapping stitch.

3 Open the body fabric out flat and line up the arm pieces, with the center on the stitched ridge. Stitch the top edge of the arm pieces on to the body.

WOMEN IN SOCIETY

The Iroquois women attended council meetings, but in most tribes women did not join councils or become warriors. Women held a respected place in society. In many tribes, such as the Algonquan, people traced their descent through their mother. When a man married, he left his home to live with his wife's family.

DISPLAYS OF WEALTH

Potlatch ceremonies could last for several days. The gathering was a big feast celebrated by tribes on the Northwest Coast. Gifts were exchanged. The status of a tribe was judged by the value of the gifts.

IN COMMAND

This chief comes from the Kainah group of Blackfoot Indians. The Kainah were also known by Europeans as the Blood Indians because of the red face paint they wore. The Blackfoot headdress had feathers that stood upright as opposed to the Sioux bonnet which sloped backwards sometimes, with trailing eagle feathers.

FEATHER PIPE OF PEACE

North American Indians had a long tradition of smoking pipes. Plants were often smoked for religious and ritual reasons. Early peace talks involved passing around a pipe for all to smoke to show they had good intentions of keeping agreements.

4 Fold the fabric in half again to see the shirt's shape. Now stitch up the undersides of the sleeves. The sides of the shirt were usually not sewn together.

5 Your shirt is ready to decorate. Cut out strips and triangles of felt and glue them on to the shirt. Make fringes by cutting into one side of a felt strip.

6 Make fake hair pieces by cutting 3 in lengths of black thread and tying them together in bunches. Wind red thread tightly around the top, as here.

7 Glue or sew the fake hair (or scalplocks) on to your shirt. You can follow the pattern we used as shown in the picture (top), or create your own.

Survival of a Tribal Tradition

Some tribal societies have had to fight to hold on to their social structure and traditions. The North American Indian culture was nearly wiped out forever. From the 1600s onward, settlers from Europe took over the land of North America and imposed their own laws. By 1900 the population of tribes north of Mexico had dropped from just below three million to 400,000.

The foreign settlers formed the United States of America at the end of the 1700s, but did not regard the native tribes as "Americans." Over the next 200 years, the US Government moved the Native American peoples from their homelands to areas of land known as reserves or reservations. About 300 US federal reservations still exist today, some for a single tribe, others as home to a number of groups.

In the 1900s, Indians became more politically active. Tribes began to demand financial compensation for lost land. The Cherokees were awarded $15 million. Today, many reservations are governed by the tribes, although the US Government still controls a lot of surviving Indian land. Since 1970, tribes have been allowed to run their reservation schools and teach ancestral history.

MODERN CEREMONIES
This couple are joining other American Indian descendants at a powwow (tribal gathering). The meetings are popular because of a recent surge of interest in the culture of the tribes. Powwows give the people a chance to dress in traditional costume, speak their native language and learn more about their tribal history.

TRIBAL PROTEST
In July 1978 these American Indians walked for five months to Washington from their reservations to protest to Congress. At protest meetings, leaders read from a list of 400 treaties – promises that the United States had made and broken. For years, many tribes tried to get back land taken from them. In 1992, Navajo and Hopi tribes were given back 1.8 million acres of their land in Northern Arizona to be divided between the tribes.

SODA BAR STOP
A Seminole family enjoy sodas in 1948 in a Miami store. Tribes gradually adapted to the American ways of life, but some kept their own customs and dress. Seminoles were forced from Florida to Oklahoma in 1878. Almost 300 refused to leave the Everglades and around 2,000 live there today.

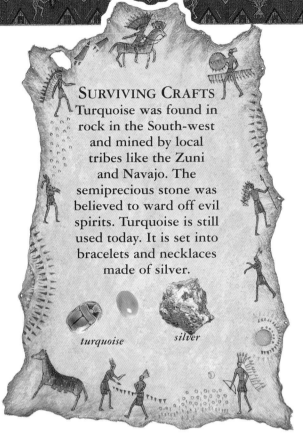

SURVIVING CRAFTS

Turquoise was found in rock in the South-west and mined by local tribes like the Zuni and Navajo. The semiprecious stone was believed to ward off evil spirits. Turquoise is still used today. It is set into bracelets and necklaces made of silver.

turquoise　　*silver*

THE TOURIST TRAIL

A traditional Inuit scene of snowshoes propped outside an igloo. Most people in Alaska and Greenland live in modern, centrally heated homes. However, the ancient skills of building temporary shelters from ice bricks still survive. They are passed down to each generation and occasionally used by hunters or tourists keen to experience North American Indian customs.

CHEERLEADING CHIEF

Dressed in full ceremonial costume, this North American Indian helps conduct celebrations at a football stadium. It is a way of raising awareness of the existence of tribes. The cheerleading is not far removed from a war chief's tribal role of encouraging warriors in battle.

STITCHING THE PAST

Traditional American Indian crafts are still made today. The method of curing hides has remained the same. No chemicals are used during the tanning process and the scraping is still done by hand. However, styles of the crafts had already changed to suit the European market in the 1600s when traders brought in new materials.

TRADITIONAL SKILLS

An Indian craftsman produces beautiful jewelry in silver and turquoise. Zuni and Navajo people were among the finest jewelry makers in this style. Other tribes, such as the Crow, are famous for their beadwork.

Glossary

A

ancestor A member of the same family who died long ago.

Anno Domini (AD) A system used to calculate dates after the supposed year of Christ's birth. AD dates are written before the date (e.g. AD521).

archaeologist Someone who studies ancient ruins and artefacts to learn about the past.

aristocracy A ruling class of wealthy, privileged people, or government by such people.

artefact An object that has been preserved from the past.

B

barbarians Wild, rough and uncivilized people. The word was invented by the ancient Greeks for people who did not speak their language or follow their lifestyle.

barter The exchange of goods, one for the other.

Before Christ (BC) A system used to calculate dates before the supposed year of Christ's birth. Dates are calculated in reverse (e.g. 200BC is longer ago than 1BC). The letters BC follow the date (e.g. 455BC).

Buddhism World religion founded in ancient India by the Buddha in the 6th century BC.

C

cavalry Soldiers on horseback.

citizen A free person with the right to vote.

city-state A center of government based on a city and controlling surrounding lands.

civil servant Official who carries out administrative duties for a government.

civilization A society that makes advances in arts, sciences, technology, law and government.

clan A group of people related to one another through their ancestors or by marriage.

colony A group of people who settle in another land, but still keep links with their own country.

Confucianism Western name for the teachings of Kong Fuzi (Confucius), which call for social order and respect for one's family and ancestors.

conscription A term of service to the State, in which people have to work as laborers or soldiers.

consul A leader of the Roman Republic.

currency Form of exchange for goods such as money.

D

daimyo A Japanese noble or warlord.

Danegeld Money paid to Vikings by English or French rulers to prevent their lands being attacked.

democracy Government by the many, in which every citizen has the right to vote and hold public office.

descendant Person who is descended from an individual or group of people who lived earlier.

dictator A ruler with complete and unrestricted power.

drought A long period with no rain.

druid A Celtic priest.

dynasty A period of rule by the same royal family.

E

empire A group of lands ruled or governed by a single country.

estate A large amount of land, houses and farms, usually owned by a single person or group.

evolution A gradual change, maybe over thousands of years, during which the thing that is changing becomes more complex.

F

federal Central government of a federation (a group).

feud A long-standing quarrel, especially between two families.

G

garrison A band of soldiers living in a particular place.

government The way in which a country or state is ruled.

guilds Groups of skilled workers who check quality standards, train young people and look after old and sick members.

H

hunter-gatherer A person who hunts wild animals and gathers plants for food.

I

immigrants People who come to live in a land from other countries.

imperial Relating to the rule of an emperor or empress.

indigenous Originating from a country, native.

inscribed Letters or pictures carved on stone or another hard material.

irrigation The process of taking water to dry land for crops.

Islam The Muslim faith.

K

Koran Sacred book of Islam.

L

lacquer A shiny varnish, made from the sap of trees.

legion A section of the Roman Army that was made up only of Roman citizens.

legislation Making laws.

litter A portable bed or chair on which wealthy and privileged people were carried.

M

magistrate An imperial officer of justice, similar to a local judge.

mercenary A soldier who fights for an army for money, not because it is the army of his own country.

merchant A person who buys and sells goods for a profit.

metic A foreigner resident in ancient Athens.

migration The movement of people to other regions either permanently or at specific times of the year.

mit'a Conscripted labor, owed to the Inca state as a form of tax.

monarchy Government by a king or queen.

monsoon Winds that blow at a particular season of the year in south Asia, bringing heavy rain.

N

nobles People who are high in social rank.

nomadic People who move from one area to another to find food, better land or to follow herds.

Normans Descendants of the Vikings who settled in a part of northern France (Normandy).

O

oligarchy Government by a group of rich and powerful people.

omen A sign of good or bad fortune in the future.

overseer A supervisor or boss.

P

pagan Pre-Christian worshipping of the old gods of Nature.

parasite In Celtic times, the low-ranking follower of a chieftain.

peasant A poor country dweller.

plate-armor Protective clothing made of overlapping plates of metal.

plebeian A member of the (free) common people of ancient Rome.

politics The art and science of government (from *polis*, city state).

prehistoric Belonging to the time before written records were made.

priest An official who performs sacrifices and other religious rituals.

R

regent Someone who rules a country on behalf of another person.

republic A country that is not ruled by a king, but by representatives elected by citizens.

rites Solemn procedures normally carried out for a religious purpose or as part of a ceremony.

ritual A procedure or series of actions that is often religious.

S

sacrifice The killing of a living thing in honor of the gods.

samurai Highly trained Japanese warriors.

senate The law-making assembly of ancient Rome.

shaman A medicine man or woman believed to have powers to heal and contact spirits.

society All the classes of people living in a particular community or country.

status symbols Signs of wealth and power.

stela A tall stone pillar on which important records in words or pictures were inscribed.

T

tax Goods, money or services paid to a government.

tribe A group of families who are loyal to a chief.

tribute Taxes paid in goods by conquered people.

tyranny Government by a cruel ruler.

W

warlord A man with a private army who controls a large region or territory by force.

Index